THE SALSA IS HOT

Workbook

WILLIAM P. PICKETT
Passaic High School

To my brothers, John and Ray, and my sister, Mary Jane

The Salsa Is Hot Workbook

Pearson Education, 10 Bank Street, White Plains, NY 10606

Vice president, director of publishing: *Allen Ascher*
Editorial director: *Louisa Hellegers*
Acquisitions editor: *Laura Le Dréan*
Senior development manager: *Penny Laporte*
Development editor: *Janet Johnston*
Vice president, director of design and production: *Rhea Banker*
Associate director of electronic production: *Aliza Greenblatt*
Director of manufacturing: *Patrice Fraccio*
Production manager: *Ray Keating*
Executive managing editor: *Linda Moser*
Senior production editor: *Virginia Bernard*
Associate production editor: *Sylvia Dare*
Cover design adaptation: *Paula D. Williams*
Associate digital layout manager: *Paula D. Williams*
Text art: *Don Martinetti*

ISBN: 0-13-020430-7

1 2 3 4 5 6 7 8 9 10–BAH–04 03 02 01 00

Contents

Preface

Purpose

The purpose of *The Salsa Is Hot Workbook* is to increase a student's reading, speaking, listening, and writing skills. The exercises in the workbook also reinforce and expand the vocabulary of *The Salsa Is Hot*. The exercises give students an opportunity to work with others and independently, sometimes reviewing the dialogs and stories of *The Salsa*, and sometimes using new material.

Content

Every lesson of the workbook begins with True–False or comprehension questions that review a dialog or story of *The Salsa*. The next section reviews the vocabulary of the dialog or story. Then the lesson features a new dialog, or a summary of a dialog from *The Salsa*, or a summary of a story in dialog form.

After that come a variety of exercises. Some have the students write their own dialogs and stories. There are also sharing-information sections to increase a student's fluency, and dictation exercises to improve listening comprehension. Each chapter ends with a matching exercise to review and reinforce the vocabulary of *The Salsa* and the workbook.

Use

The exercises in the workbook can be used immediately after finishing a dialog or story of *The Salsa*, or they can be used after completing a chapter. Students can use the workbook in class and at home.

Word List and Answer Key

There is a word list at the end of the workbook. The list includes the words used in the word-review exercises, the new dialogs, and the matching exercises. A separate booklet contains an answer key to the workbook.

Acknowledgments

I wish to thank Laura Le Dréan, my acquisitions editor, for her assistance and encouragement in writing this workbook. I also wish to thank Janet Johnston, Penny Laporte, and Virginia Bernard for editing the workbook.

I am grateful to Don Martinetti, who did the art work. His lively illustrations have added much to the workbook.

I wish to thank my wife, Dorothy, for reviewing the workbook and for her many suggestions and insights. They have improved the workbook. I am also grateful to my son, Edward, for his helpful comments.

1

Jobs

Good Tips

Reread the dialog "Good Tips" (page 3 of **The Salsa Is Hot**) before doing the dialog and word reviews.

DIALOG REVIEW

If the sentence is true, write **T***. If it's false, write* **F** *and change it to a true statement.*

1. _____ Ling is going to a Mexican restaurant to eat.

   _____

2. _____ She has an easy job.

   _____

3. _____ She's on her feet a lot.

   _____

4. _____ Her pay is good.

   _____

5. _____ The customers tip Ling well.

   _____

6. _____ She thinks the customers tip her well because she's pretty.

   _____

7. _____ She's smart.

   _____

WORD REVIEW

Complete the sentences with these words.

friendly	waitress	tough	imagine	tip

1. It's _____ to stop smoking.

2. I always give the barber a big _____.

3. You'll like Jessica. She's very _____.

4. Dan has a new job and makes a lot more. You can _____ how happy he is.

5. Our _____ is slow.

| low | customers | smart | too | polite |

6. Gina is an honor student. She's _____.

7. Our house is small. That's why our taxes are _____.

8. It's important to teach children to be _____.

9. We get a lot of _____ on Saturday.

10. Pedro likes Latin music, and I do _____.

A BASKETBALL PLAYER

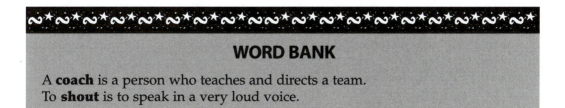

WORD BANK

A **coach** is a person who teaches and directs a team.
To **shout** is to speak in a very loud voice.

Complete the dialog with these words and practice it with a partner.

until	shoot	shouts	team	coach	practice	short

Marie and Abdul are high-school students.

Marie: Where are you going?

Abdul: To the gym. I'm on the basketball _____.

Marie: Really? Aren't you a little _____?

Abdul: Yes, but I pass and _____ well.

Marie: You must love the game.

Abdul: I do, but _____ is tough.

Marie: Why?

Abdul: We run a lot, and it's long.

Marie: How long?

Abdul: Three hours. I don't get home _____ seven.

Marie: Is your _____ good?

Abdul: Very, but he _____ a lot.

WRITING A DIALOG

Work with a partner and create your own dialog. Give your dialog a title.

_____

A: Where are you going?

B: To _____. I _____.

A: _____

B: _____

A: _____

B: _____

A: _____

B: _____

ABOUT ME

Complete these sentences.

1. After school (work) I _____.

2. I _____ school (work).

3. I _____ well.

4. I _____ a lot.

5. I think it's tough to _____.

6. I am _____ tall.

7. I think _____ polite.

8. I imagine I _____.

Baby-Sitting

Reread the dialog "Baby-Sitting" (page 6 of **The Salsa Is Hot**) before doing the dialog and word reviews.

DIALOG REVIEW

Answer these questions about the dialog. Use your own ideas to answer the last question.

1. What does Ken want Pam to do? _____

2. Why can't she go? _____

3. Why does she baby-sit? _____

4. How much does she make? _____

5. Do Pam and Ken think that's a lot of money? _____

6. What does Ken want to do? _____

7. Why can't Ken keep Pam company? _____

8. Why do you think Mrs. Franco doesn't allow Pam to have her friends visit when she baby-sits? _____

_____

WORD REVIEW

Complete the sentences with these words.

sorry	have got to	wrong	boring	besides

1. Something is _____ with our TV, and I can't fix it.

2. Amy got a 50 on her math test. It was hard. _____, she didn't study.

3. I'm _____ that you're not feeling well.

4. Hiroshi loves baseball, but I think it's _____.

5. I _____ wash the clothes.

| company | better | losing | later | allowed |

6. I'm going to play basketball now and do my homework _____.

7. When we have _____, we put the dog in the yard.

8. The high school is _____ its principal. She's moving to Texas.

9. Students aren't _____ to eat in the classrooms.

10. It's _____ to play a sport than to watch it. `

COMPANY TOMORROW

WORD BANK

To **bake** is to cook something in an oven.
Horrible means very bad.
The rest means what remains.

Complete the dialog with these words and practice it with a partner.

throw out	kind	horrible	completely
bake	favorite	rest	

Kevin and Emily are married.

Kevin: Do you want to go to the movies tonight?

Emily: We can't. We're having company tomorrow.

Kevin: That's right. I _____ forgot. Your mother and sister are coming.

Emily: Yes, and I want to _____ a pie for them tonight.

Kevin: What _____ of pie?

Emily: Apple.

Kevin: Great! That's my _____.

Emily: And we have to clean the family room.

Kevin: Why? What's wrong with it?

Emily: Those old magazines and newspapers look _____.

Kevin: Maybe, but you know I like to save them.

Emily: OK, but _____ what you can. And put the _____ in the basement.

How Often and How Interesting?

Read the list of activities and next to each write how often you do them and how interesting they are for you. In the "How often?" column, write a lot, sometimes, almost never, *or* never. *In the "How interesting?" column, write* very interesting, interesting, OK, boring, *or* very boring.

		How often?	How interesting?
1.	listening to music	_____	_____
2.	jogging	_____	_____
3.	watching a soccer game	_____	_____
4.	reading a magazine	_____	_____
5.	watching the news on TV	_____	_____
6.	shopping	_____	_____
7.	playing cards	_____	_____
8.	reading a library book	_____	_____

SHARING INFORMATION

Discuss these questions with a partner.

1. Name some things students are usually not allowed to do in a classroom.

2. Name something not in the list on the previous page that you find boring.

3. Name some things that you have got to do.

4. Do you like pie? If so, what is your favorite pie?

5. What is your favorite dessert?

6. Do you like to save things? If so, what?

7. What's the problem with saving too many things?

A Police Officer

Reread the dialog "A Police Officer" (page 9 of **The Salsa Is Hot**) before doing the dialog and word reviews.

DIALOG REVIEW

*If the sentence is true, write **T**. If it's false, write **F** and change it to a true statement.*

1. _____ Tamika tells her dad that she wants to be a police officer.
   _____

2. _____ She is kidding him.
   _____

3. _____ She knows how dangerous police work is.
   _____

4. _____ Her dad doesn't want her to be a police officer.
   _____

5. _____ He suggests that she be a teacher.
   _____

6. _____ She listens to him and changes her mind.
   _____

7. _____ He is going to let her try to be a police officer.
   _____

WORD REVIEW

Complete the sentences with these words.

serious	let	of course	officers	still

1. _____, I'll go to your party.

2. Is Rita _____ watching TV?

3. Henry had a _____ talk with his son.

4. There are two _____ in the police car.

5. My parents won't _____ me go to the concert.

| kids | dangerous | like | have to | trying |

6. I _____ return this book to the library.

7. Driving very fast is _____.

8. Tiffany is _____ to find a better job.

9. Why don't we move to a warm state, _____ Florida.

10. Don't believe everything Wayne says. He _____ a lot.

FORTY ON A TEST

WORD BANK

A **bit** means a small amount.
To **fool around** is to act in a playful manner.
To **behave** is to act well—to act the way you should.
To **fail** is to not pass—to do work that is not satisfactory.

Complete the dialog with these words and practice it with a partner.

wrong	behave	failing	fools around
weak	better	bit	

Jim is talking to his mother.

Jim: Mom, I have something to tell you.

Mom: What is it?

Jim: My algebra teacher is going to call you.

Mom: Why? Are you in trouble?

Jim: A little _____.

Mom: What's _____?

Jim: My teacher says I talk too much.

Mom: Do you?

Jim: Yes, but everyone _____ in his class.

Mom: I don't care what the others do. You have to _____.

Jim: I also got a 40 on a test. You know I'm _____ in math.

Mom: I don't want to hear any excuses. Are you _____?

Jim: Yes, I am.

Mom: I'm very unhappy about this.

Jim: I understand. I'll try to do _____.

WRITING A DIALOG

Work with a partner and create your own dialog. Give your dialog a title.

_____

A: _____, I have something to tell you.

B: What is it?

A: _____

B: _____

A: _____

B: _____

A: _____

B: _____

SHARING INFORMATION

Discuss or complete these statements and questions.

1. Name some things, actions, and jobs that are dangerous.
2. It's safe to _____.
3. Of course, _____.
4. I'm unhappy about _____.
5. Name things you're trying to do.
6. How often do (did) you fool around in class? Often? Sometimes? Rarely? Never?
7. Do you have a subject you're weak in? If so, what is it?
8. Give as many excuses as you can think of for not doing well on a test.

Delivering Mail

Reread the dialog "Delivering Mail" (page 12 of **The Salsa Is Hot**) before doing the dialog and word reviews.

DIALOG REVIEW

Answer these questions about the dialog. Use your own ideas to answer the last question.

1. What does Doug think of his salary? _____

2. How does he like working outdoors? _____

3. How does he feel about working in rain and snow? _____

    _____

4. Do dogs bother him a lot? _____

5. What's the best thing about his job? _____

6. Why doesn't he have to worry about losing his job? _____

    _____

7. What is Ashley thinking about doing? _____

8. Do you think Ashley will apply for the job? Explain your answer.

    _____

    _____

WORD REVIEW

Complete the sentences with these words.

bother	deliver	fire	rushing	bet

1. The company is losing money. It's going to _____ some workers.

2. It's been a long day. I _____ you're tired.

3. Will it _____ you if I play the piano?

4. Carl is _____ to finish his test before the bell rings.

5. They're going to _____ the pizza to our house.

14

hate	applying	outdoors	secure	letter carrier

6. Dianne is _____ to three colleges.

7. It's important that children feel _____ in school.

8. I _____ to ask you for money.

9. The mail didn't come yet. Our _____ is late.

10. Tell the children to play _____.

HELPING PEOPLE

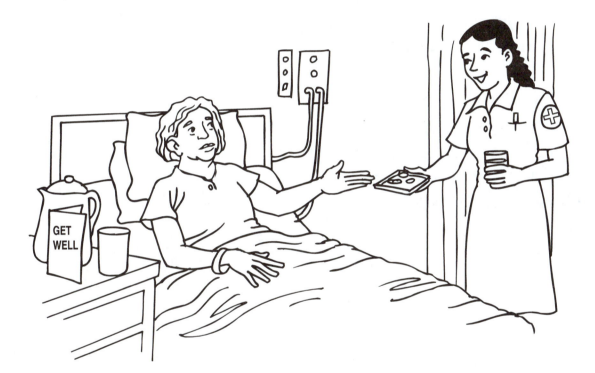

WORD BANK

A **patient** is a person receiving care in a hospital or from a doctor.
Anything that makes us tired is **tiring.**
A **mistake** is an error—something that is not correct.
Worst is the superlative of *bad.* (*bad, worse, worst*)
Reports and other things one must write are **paperwork**.

Complete the dialog with these words and practice it with a partner.

tiring	paperwork	unpleasant	mistake
example	patients	worst	

Andy and Beth are friends. She's a nurse.

Andy: Do you like being a nurse?

Beth: I love it, but there are problems.

Andy: For _____?

Beth: Doctors who are _____.

Andy: And what about the _____?

Beth: Most are nice, but a few aren't.

Andy: Is your job _____?

Beth: Very. I'm on my feet a lot, and I'm always busy.

Andy: And you have to know what you're doing.

Beth: Yes, a _____ can cost a life.

Andy: What's the best thing about your job?

Beth: Helping people who need me.

Andy: And the _____ thing?

Beth: _____! I hate it!

SHARING INFORMATION

Discuss these questions with a partner.

1. Some doctors are kind to their patients, but not to the nurses. Why is that?
2. The adjective *unpleasant* can describe many things, for example, unpleasant weather. Name some other things that can be unpleasant.
3. Can you think of an example where a nurse's mistake could cost a life?
4. What's the best thing about your job (or being a student)?
5. What's the worst thing?
6. Nursing is a helping profession—a profession in which your work helps people. Name some other helping professions.
7. Give some examples of the paperwork that nurses, teachers, and police officers have to do.

COMPLETING A STORY

Work with a partner and write your own story. Give your story a title.

_____

Denise is a teacher at _____ . She likes her job, and most of her students _____ , but _____ .

The best thing about her job is _____ .

She also _____ .

There are, however, two things she doesn't like about her job. First, _____ .

Second, _____ .

From Quito to Jersey City

*Reread the story "From Quito to Jersey City" (page 15 of **The Salsa Is Hot**) before doing the Story Review, Word Review, and Word and Story Review.*

STORY REVIEW

*If the sentence is true, write **T**. If it's false, write **F** and change it to a true statement*

1. _____ Quito is near the equator and is very hot.
   _____

2. _____ Quito is a beautiful city.
   _____

3. _____ Juan had a job in Quito.
   _____

4. _____ He hoped to make a lot of money in the United States.
   _____

5. _____ He lived with his cousin in Jersey City.
   _____

6. _____ He liked the hot weather in Jersey City.
   _____

7. _____ He knew a lot of English.
   _____

8. _____ He tried to get a job in a factory.
   _____

WORD REVIEW

Complete the sentences with these words.

discovered	few	peaceful	smile	hiring

1. I like to walk in the park. It's very _____.
2. Our company is _____ more workers.
3. Connnie _____ an excellent Italian restaurant.
4. Ahmad is very serious. He doesn't _____ often.
5. We have to leave in a _____ minutes.

humid	ago	find	engaged	soon

6. We're going to eat _____.

7. I can't _____ my sweater. Did you see it?

8. It gets very hot in Arizona, but it isn't _____.

9. Stacy and Jeff are only 19, but they're _____.

10. The letter carrier came an hour _____.

WORD AND STORY REVIEW

Complete the dialog with these words and practice it with a partner.

factories	smile	hiring	bet	mountains
find	equator	engaged	ago	help-wanted

Hard to Get a Job

Rosa is a friend of Juan's cousin. Juan is talking to her.

Rosa: When did you come to the United States?

Juan: Two months _____.

Rosa: Where are you from?

Juan: Quito, Ecuador. It's a few miles from the _____.

Rosa: It must be hot.

Juan: No, it's in the _____ and never gets hot.

Rosa: Do you have a job?

Juan: No, not yet.

Rosa: How much English do you know?

Juan: Very little.

Rosa: Did you try any _____?

Juan: Yes, but they weren't _____.

Rosa: Did you look at the _____ ads in the papers?

Juan: I did, but I didn't _____ anything.

Rosa: Keep looking; you'll get a job. Are you married?

Juan: No, but I'm _____ to a girl from Quito.

Rosa: I _____ you have a photo of her.

Juan: Of course. Here it is.

Rosa: She's very pretty, and she has a nice _____.

Juan: Why, thank you!

INTERVIEW

Interview a partner so you can write a story about him or her. Ask these questions and any others that will help you write an interesting story about the person. (Ask the questions in 2A if he or she is working. Ask the questions in 2B if he or she is a student.) As you interview, write notes on the lines below the questions.

1. What country and city are you from? Describe the city, its size, its weather, etc. When did you come to the United States? Why did you come? Where are you living now?

   _____

   _____

   _____

2a. Are you working? Where? What kind of work? Do you like your work? If you're a homemaker, describe your work at home. If you are unemployed, what kind of work would you like to get? _____

   _____

   _____

   _____

2b. Are you a student? Where do you go to school? What is your best subject? Which is the most difficult for you? Do you like your school? Do you like your teachers? Why or why not? _____

   _____

   _____

3. Tell me a little about the things you like to do, and how often you do them. Do you like to watch TV? read? play sports? dance? go to parties? _____

   _____

   _____

   _____

   _____

WRITING

Write a composition of three paragraphs about the person you interviewed. In the first paragraph, use the answers to the questions in number 1; in the second paragraph, use the answers to the questions in number 2A or 2B; in the third paragraph, use the answers to the questions in number 3.

A Newcomer

_____

_____

_____

_____

_____

_____

_____

_____

_____

_____

_____

_____

_____

_____

_____

_____

_____

_____

_____

_____

Working in a Diner

Reread the story "Working in a Diner" (page 19 of **The Salsa Is Hot**) before doing the Story Review, Word Review, and Word and Story Review.

STORY REVIEW

If the sentence is true, write **T**. If it's false, write **F** and change it to a true statement.

1. _____ Juan works at an expensive retaurant.

   _____

2. _____ He makes enough to pay his bills.

   _____

3. _____ He goes to the park to watch his cousin play soccer.

   _____

4. _____ Juan and his cousin eat and play in the park.

   _____

5. _____ They go for a walk after they play soccer.

   _____

6. _____ Juan feels that the United States is his country because it's a country of immigrants.

   _____

7. _____ He writes to Sonia every week.

   _____

8. _____ He is saving money to buy a house.

   _____

WORD REVIEW

Complete the sentences with these words.

reminded	along	statue	enough	arrived

1. The train _____ 20 minutes late.
2. There is a _____ of Benjamin Franklin in the museum.
3. My wife _____ me to buy stamps.
4. Do we have _____ time to stop and visit our friends?
5. The flowers _____ the side of the house are pretty.

immigrants	rent	finally	so	miss

6. We're going to _____ a movie and watch it after dinner.

7. Karol is saving money _____ he can visit Poland.

8. Many of the students in our class are _____.

9. The waitress is _____ bringing our food.

10. My girlfriend went to Mexico for her vacation. I _____ her.

WORD AND STORY REVIEW

Complete the dialog with these words and practice it with a partner.

at least	view	tough	miss	bills
expensive	diner	soccer	so	phone

The Kitchen Is Hot

Juan is talking to his sister-in-law, Blanca.

Blanca: Where are you working, Juan?

Juan: At a _____. I work in the kitchen.

Blanca: That's _____ work.

Juan: It sure is. The kitchen is very hot.

Blanca: Well, _____ you have a job.

Juan: True, and I'm able to pay my _____ and save a little.

Blanca: What do you do on your days off?

Juan: On Sunday afternoon, I play _____ with my cousin and some friends.

Blanca: Where?

Juan: At Liberty State Park.

Blanca: Isn't that the park with a _____ of the Statue of Liberty?

Juan: Exactly. I also _____ Sonia every Sunday night.

Blanca: You must _____ her.

Juan: Yes, a lot. We talk for more than an hour.

Blanca: Isn't that a little _____?

Juan: It is, and I'm trying to save every penny I can.

Blanca: To buy a car?

Juan: No, _____ we can rent a nice apartment when Sonia comes.

SHARING INFORMATION

Discuss these questions with a partner.

1. What are some good things about eating in a diner?

2. How many cousins do you have?

3. Do you see them often?

4. Are salaries in the United States higher than in your country? much higher?

5. Is food more expensive in the United States or in your country? clothing? cars? gas? houses? taking a taxi?

6. Do (or did) you ever play soccer? a lot?

7. Do you ever watch soccer on TV? often?

8. Name as many things as you can that people rent.

MATCHING

Match the words in Column A with their definitions or descriptions in Column B. Print the letters on the blank lines.

	Column A	Column B
_____	1. behave	**A.** a small amount
_____	2. horrible	**B.** an error
_____	3. bit	**C.** to not pass
_____	4. shout	**D.** to act in a playful manner
_____	5. paperwork	**E.** a person receiving care from a doctor
_____	6. fail	**F.** to speak in a very loud voice
_____	7. patient (noun)	**G.** very bad
_____	8. mistake	**H.** a person who directs a team
_____	9. coach	**I.** reports one must write
_____	10. fool around	**J.** to act well

2

Sports

Basketball or Math

Reread the dialog "Basketball or Math" (page 25 of **The Salsa Is Hot**) before doing the dialog and word reviews.

DIALOG REVIEW

*If the sentence is true, write **T**. If it's false, write **F** and change it to a true statement.*

1. _____ Kristin is going to the park.

_____

2. _____ She invites Brenda to go with her.

_____

3. _____ Brenda doesn't want to go to the park.

_____

4. _____ The math test is going to be hard.

_____

5. _____ Brenda is going to study later.

_____

6. _____ Kristin doesn't have any homework.

_____

7. _____ Brenda says she's going to study hard.

_____

WORD REVIEW

Complete the sentences with these words.

have to	lucky	tough	too	worry

1. I _____ about Sam. He drinks a lot.

2. Nancy is _____. She has a good job and a nice family.

3. Jason isn't going to run today. It's _____ hot.

4. I _____ look for a job.

5. That's a _____ question. I can't answer it.

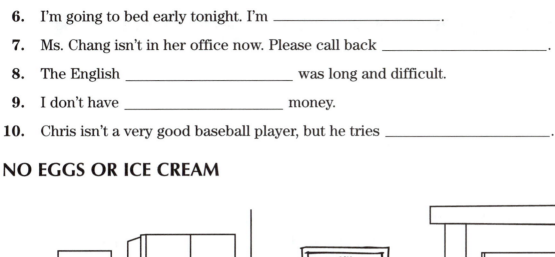

later	any	tired	hard	test

6. I'm going to bed early tonight. I'm _____.

7. Ms. Chang isn't in her office now. Please call back _____.

8. The English _____ was long and difficult.

9. I don't have _____ money.

10. Chris isn't a very good baseball player, but he tries _____.

NO EGGS OR ICE CREAM

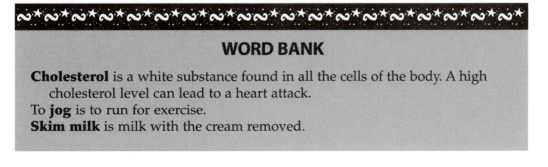

WORD BANK

Cholesterol is a white substance found in all the cells of the body. A high cholesterol level can lead to a heart attack.

To **jog** is to run for exercise.

Skim milk is milk with the cream removed.

Complete the dialog with these words and practice it with a partner.

cholesterol	exercise	blood	less	jog	wrong	skim

Gina and Mark are friends.

Gina: Where are you going?

Mark: To the hospital for a _____ test.

Gina: Is something _____?

Mark: My _____ is high.

Gina: What are you doing about it?

Mark: I'm eating _____ meat and drinking _____ milk.

Gina: What about butter?

Mark: No butter, eggs, or ice cream for me.

Gina: Are you getting more _____?

Mark: Yes, I _____ every day.

Gina: That should help.

Mark: I hope so.

WRITING A DIALOG

Work with a partner and create your own dialog. Give your dialog a title.

_____

A: Where are you going?

B: To _____.

A: _____

B: _____

A: _____

B: _____

A: _____

B: _____

DICTATION

1. *Listen while the teacher or your partner reads the dialog without stopping.* **Don't write anything.**
2. *The teacher or your partner will read the dialog a second time, pausing after the missing lines.* **Write in the missing lines.**
3. *The teacher or your partner will read the dialog a third time.* **Check your work.**

Gina: Where are you going?

Mark: _____

Gina: Is something wrong?

Mark: _____

Gina: What are you doing about it?

Mark: _____

Gina: What about butter?

Mark: _____

Football

Reread the dialog "Football" (page 28 of **The Salsa Is Hot**) before doing the dialog and word reviews.

DIALOG REVIEW

Answer these questions about the dialog. Use your own ideas to answer the last question.

1. What sport does Tony want to play? _____

2. Why doesn't his mom want him to play football? _____

3. How does Tony say he can get hurt? _____

4. How much does he weigh? _____

5. Why doesn't he have to be big to play football? _____

6. What does his mom suggest he do? _____

7. Why doesn't he want to play soccer? _____

8. Tony's mom allows him to play football. Do you think she is right? Explain your answer.

   _____

   _____

WORD REVIEW

Complete the sentences with these words.

dangerous	weighs	hurt	safe	crossed

1. Jackie fell and _____ her back.

2. It's _____ to drive when it's snowing hard.

3. The plane _____ the Atlantic Ocean in four hours.

4. My sister isn't fat, but she _____ more than I do.

5. Don't play in the street. Play in the school yard. It's _____ there.

30

pounds	go ahead	like	enough	sorry

6. I'm _____ I can't go to the dance, but I'm working.

7. Cook something we all eat, _____ spaghetti.

8. I'm going to the store to get bread and five _____ of sugar.

9. Sam wants to be a doctor, but he's not smart _____.

10. I think we should _____ and buy a new car.

GETTING A MOTORCYCLE

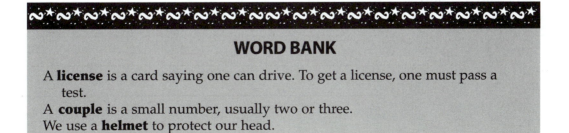

WORD BANK

A **license** is a card saying one can drive. To get a license, one must pass a
   test.
A **couple** is a small number, usually two or three.
We use a **helmet** to protect our head.

Complete the dialog with these words and practice it with a partner.

ago	besides	serious	wear	license	helmet	couple

Tim is talking to his father.

Tim: Dad, I want to get a motorcycle.

Dad: You've got to be kidding.

Tim: No, I'm very _____.

Dad: When did you get your driver's _____?

Tim: Six months _____.

Dad: And now you want to to learn to drive a motorcycle?

Tim: That's right.

Dad: Why don't you wait a _____ of years?

Tim: I'm 18. That's old enough.

Dad: If that's what you want, OK, but you have to do one thing.

Tim: What's that?

Dad: Always _____ a _____.

Tim: That's no problem. _____, it's the law.

SENTENCE COMPLETION

Complete these sentences.

1. I think that riding a motorcycle is _____.

2. I want to _____, but I can't because _____.

    _____.

3. _____ is not my game, but I like to play _____.

4. You can easily get hurt _____.

5. I'm sorry, but I can't _____.

6. I don't have enough _____ to _____.

7. You don't have to be big to _____.

SHARING INFORMATION

Discuss these questions with a partner.

1. Is it very dangerous to ride a motorcycle? Explain your answer.

2. Do you know anyone who rides one? If so, who? Is he or she young?

3. Why do you think some people like to ride a motorcycle?

4. Do you have a driver's license?

5. If not, do you plan to get one?

6. It's important to wear a helmet when riding a motorcycle. How important is it to wear a helmet when riding a bicycle?

7. Does your state have a law that motorcyle riders must wear a helmet?

8. In what sports do players have to wear a helmet?

Hunting

*Reread the dialog "Hunting" (page 31 of **The Salsa Is Hot**) before doing the dialog and word reviews.*

DIALOG REVIEW

*If the sentence is true, write **T**. If it's false, write **F** and change it to a true statement.*

1. _____ Alicia wants to go hunting with Ray and Mike.
   _____

2. _____ The big reason Ray hunts is to get fresh air and exercise.
   _____

3. _____ He goes hunting in a woods about 20 miles from where he lives.
   _____

4. _____ Alicia doesn't think people should hunt.
   _____

5. _____ She believes it's OK to kill cows for food.
   _____

6. _____ Ray hunts just for fun.
   _____

7. _____ He doesn't think before he shoots.
   _____

WORD REVIEW

Complete the sentences with these words.

believes in	outdoors	shoot	beef	exercise

1. The doctor wants me to eat less _____.

2. The children are playing _____.

3. Craig doesn't get much _____. He's lazy.

4. Our history teacher _____ giving a lot of homework.

5. Someone tried to _____ the president.

fun	woods	hunt	season	just

6. You have to be careful when you _____.

7. The parade was _____. I'm glad I went.

8. I watch TV _____ at night.

9. It's cool in the _____.

10. The baseball _____ is very long.

WOW! THAT'S HOT!

WORD BANK

A **degree** is a measure of heat.
Humid air has a lot of water in it.
Water moves across the surface of the ocean in **waves**.

Complete the dialog with these words and practice it with a partner.

humid	breeze	swimsuit	temperature
waves	degrees	beach	

Stan is Donna's brother.

Stan: What's the _____?

Donna: It's 98 _____.

Stan: Wow! That's hot!

Donna: And it's very _____.

Stan: I can't take this heat.

Donna: Let's go to the _____.

Stan: Good idea. We'll be cooler there.

Donna: And there's always a _____.

Stan: Yes, and we can go swimming in the ocean.

Donna: I love the big _____.

Stan: I'll drive. We can leave in five minutes.

Donna: Good. Don't forget a _____ and a towel.

WRITING A DIALOG

Work with a partner and create your own dialog. Give your dialog a title.

_____

A: What's the temperature?

B: It's _____ degrees.

A: _____

B: _____

A: _____

B: _____

A: _____

B: _____

SHARING INFORMATION

Discuss these questions with a partner.

1. Which is worse for you—very hot weather or very cold weather?

2. Is the summer hotter where you lived in your country or where you live now?

3. Which do you like better, swimming in the ocean or in a pool?
   Explain your answer.

4. Do you think people spend more time outdoors in your country or in the United States?
   Explain your answer.

5. Do you eat much beef?

6. Is there a problem with eating a lot of beef? If so, what is the problem?

7. What is a veggieburger? Why do some people eat them?

8. Name something you believe in.

A Hockey Star

Reread the dialog "A Hockey Star" (page 34 of **The Salsa Is Hot**) before doing the dialog and word reviews.

DIALOG REVIEW

Answer these questions about the dialog. Use your own ideas to answer the last question.

1. What news does Kathy have for her mom? _____

2. What does scoring three goals tell us about Jennifer? _____

3. What problem does Betty have? _____

4. Why does she think that girls shouldn't play hockey? _____

5. What does Kathy think of her mom's opinion and why? _____

   _____

6. What does Kathy invite her mom to? _____

7. How does her mom reply to the invitation? _____

8. Do you think Betty will be proud of Jenn? Do you think she will change her mind about girls playing hockey? Explain your answers.

   _____

   _____

WORD REVIEW

Complete the sentences with these words.

news	entirely	rough	proud	guess

1. Dennis and Paula are _____ of their grandchildren.

2. Did you hear the big _____? The president is going to visit our school.

3. The football game was _____.

4. Angela didn't come to work today. I _____ she's sick.

5. No one is _____ bad.

spirit	silly	mean	next	once

6. I don't understand what you're saying. Please explain what you _____.

7. Malak visits her sister _____ a week.

8. Larry is in many school activities. He has a lot of school _____.

9. I have to go to the dentist _____ Monday.

10. Travis is very nice, but he has a lot of _____ ideas.

SELLING HOUSES

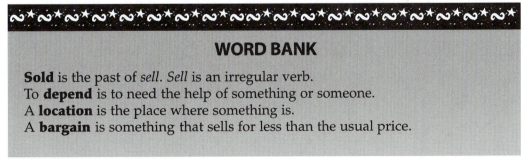

WORD BANK

Sold is the past of *sell*. *Sell* is an irregular verb.
To **depend** is to need the help of something or someone.
A **location** is the place where something is.
A **bargain** is something that sells for less than the usual price.

Complete the dialog with these words and practice it with a partner.

congratulations	bargain	sold	location
at least	still	depends	

Gary is visiting Lynn. They're cousins.

Gary: Are you _____ selling houses?

Lynn: Yes, I _____ one last week for $200,000.

Gary: _____! How much did you make?

Lynn: Three thousand dollars.

Gary: That's great. Is it hard to sell a house?

Lynn: It all _____.

Gary: On what?

Lynn: _____ is the most important thing.

Gary: Of course. People want to live in a nice area.

Lynn: And price is very important.

Gary: I guess everyone wants a _____.

Lynn: Yes, or _____ a price they can pay.

SHARING INFORMATION

Discuss these questions with a partner.

1. Many people work at selling things, for example, insurance, cars, or computers. Do you think you would be good at selling things?

2. About how much does a nice house in a nice area cost in your city?

3. The price of a house depends on its location. What else does it depend on?

4. What do you think of the location where you're living? Is it safe or dangerous? Is it nice or not so nice?

5. Most newcomers to the United States don't have enough or make enough money to buy a house. Is buying a house a dream of yours—something that you want to do very much? Explain your answer.

6. What are some of the advantages (good things) of owning a house?

7. Owning a house is expensive. What are some of the things owners have to pay for after they move into a house?

WRITING

Write two paragraphs about your dream house. In the first paragraph, describe its size, its location, its rooms, its yard. In the second paragraph, tell how much you think it will cost and how you're going to pay for it.

My Dream House

_____

_____

_____

_____

_____

_____

_____

_____

_____

_____

_____

_____

_____

_____

Roberto Clemente

Reread the story "Roberto Clemente" (page 37 of **The Salsa Is Hot**) before doing the Story Review, Word Review, and Word and Story Review.

STORY REVIEW

*If the sentence is true, write **T**. If it's false, write **F** and change it to a true statement.*

1. _____ Roberto was thin, and his arm was weak.

   _____

2. _____ Campanis discovered that Roberto was fast but couldn't hit well.

   _____

3. _____ The Dodgers paid Roberto $10,000 to sign to play for them.

   _____

4. _____ Roberto came from a large family.

   _____

5. _____ His dad worked hard and made a lot of money.

   _____

6. _____ Roberto loved baseball and played for hours.

   _____

7. _____ Roberto was happy in Montreal and liked the food there.

   _____

8. _____ The Pittsburgh Pirates were the only major-league team Roberto ever played for.

   _____

WORD REVIEW

Complete the sentences with these words.

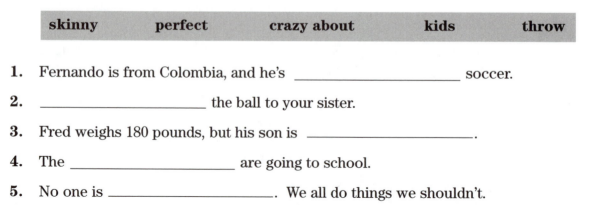

skinny	perfect	crazy about	kids	throw

1. Fernando is from Colombia, and he's _____ soccer.

2. _____ the ball to your sister.

3. Fred weighs 180 pounds, but his son is _____.

4. The _____ are going to school.

5. No one is _____. We all do things we shouldn't.

42

career	teammates	against	sent	scouts

6. My brother is _____ gun control, but I think we need more.

7. Jamal is the best basketball player in the city; _____ often come to watch him play.

8. Tom has a dangerous _____. He works for the F.B.I.

9. Peggy _____ her son to the store to get bread and milk.

10. Valerie and Nicole play volleyball for their high school. They're _____.

WORD AND STORY REVIEW

Complete the dialog with these words and practice it with a partner.

against	kids	minor-league	too	throw
send	sign	seconds	sugar-cane	contract

I Want to Play in the Majors

Al Campanis, a scout for the Brooklyn Dodgers, is talking to Roberto Clemente.

Campanis: That was a great _____ you made from center field.

Roberto: Thanks. I have a strong arm.

Campanis: And you ran 40 yards in 4.6 _____.

Roberto: That's good time.

Campanis: And you got some good hits _____ my best pitcher.

Roberto: Do you think I can play for the Dodgers?

Campanis: Yes, I'm going to offer you a _____ to play for them.

Roberto: Wonderful, but I have to talk to my parents before I _____.

Campanis: Of course. I want to talk to them _____.

Roberto: We live in Carolina, and I'm the youngest of six _____.

Campanis: What does your father do?

Roberto: He works in the _____ fields.

Campanis: We may _____ you to Montreal for a year.

Roberto: That's OK.

Campanis: Montreal is our best _____ team.

Roberto: Good, but someday I want to play in the majors.

Campanis: Don't worry. You will.

WRITING

When Roberto Clemente went to live and play baseball in Montreal, he wasn't happy. He missed his family and friends, his mother's cooking, and the warm weather of Puerto Rico.

When people go to live in a new country, they suffer "culture shock." The customs, the weather, the language, the food, and the people of the new country are so different. The newcomers miss many things, and life can be difficult.

Write two paragraphs about what you missed and what was difficult for you when you first came to the United States.

Culture Shock

_____

_____

_____

_____

_____

_____

_____

_____

_____

_____

_____

_____

_____

_____

_____

_____

Now write a paragraph about what you liked when you first came to the United States.

_____

_____

_____

_____

_____

_____

_____

_____

_____

The Hall of Fame

Reread the story "The Hall of Fame" (page 41 of **The Salsa Is Hot**) before doing the Story Review, Word Review, and Word and Story Review.

STORY REVIEW

*If the sentence is true, write **T**. If it's false, write **F** and change it to a true statement.*

1. _____ Roberto Clemente got 3,000 major-league hits.

   _____

2. _____ Many major-league players get 3,000 hits.

   _____

3. _____ Roberto was a very good right fielder and made many great catches.

   _____

4. _____ In 1966, Roberto was voted the most valuable player in the American League.

   _____

5. _____ Roberto died trying to help others.

   _____

6. _____ His plane crashed near Managua, Nicaragua.

   _____

7. _____ Soon after his death, Roberto was elected to the Baseball Hall of Fame.

   _____

8. _____ One player on the Pirates always wears number 21.

   _____

WORD REVIEW

Complete the sentences with these words.

take off	supplies	however	terrible	valuable

1. I don't feel well. _____, I'm going to work today.

2. What time does the plane _____?

3. This ring is very _____.

4. The teacher put the _____ in the gray cabinet.

5. I have a _____ cold.

46

dying	uniforms	crashed into	catch	elect

6. In many countries, children wear _____ to school.

7. I tried to _____ the ball, but it went over my head.

8. The roses were beatiful, but they're _____ now.

9. In November, we're going to _____ a new governor.

10. Steve _____ a tree as he was skiing down a mountain.

WORD AND STORY REVIEW

Complete the dialog with these words and practice it with a partner.

crashed	earthquake	die	elected	catches
retired	title	supplies	hits	terrible

A Great Person and a Great Player

Bill and José meet at a party. They're 12 years old.

Bill: Where do you go to school?

José: Roberto Clemente School.

Bill: Wasn't Roberto a great baseball player?

José: Yes, he got 3,000 major-league _____.

Bill: Wow! That's a lot.

José: And he won the batting _____ four times.

Bill: What position did he play?

José: Right field, and he made many great _____.

Bill: Didn't he _____ young?

José: Yes, his plane _____ off the coast of Puerto Rico.

Bill: That's _____.

José: He was bringing food and _____ to the people of Nicaragua.

Bill: Why?

José: There was a big _____ in Nicaragua.

Bill: Roberto was a great person and a great player.

José: That's why he was _____ to the Baseball Hall of Fame in 1972.

Bill: I didn't know that.

José: Yes, and the Pirates _____ his uniform number—21.

Bill: Your school must be proud of him.

José: Very.

SHARING INFORMATION

Discuss these questions with a partner or in a small group. Try to have a student in each group who knows something about baseball.

1. When Roberto Clemente played for Pittsburgh, there weren't a lot of Hispanic players in the major leagues. Are there many today?
2. Name as many Hispanic countries as you can that have players in the major leagues.
3. A team from Cuba came to the the United States to play the Baltimore Orioles, a major-league team. Do you think baseball will help the United States and Cuba have better relations? Explain your answer.
4. In what Asian country is baseball especially popular? Does that country have any players in the major leagues?
5. They say baseball is the national sport of the United States, but football and basketball are also popular. Many think they are more exciting. Which of these three sports do you think is the most exciting? Why?
6. A game similar to baseball (and also very different) is the national sport of England, India, and Pakistan. What is the name of that sport?
7. Baseball was a big interest of Roberto Clemente. Complete this sentence about yourself. *I am very interested in* _____.
8. What are some advantages of having different interests?

MATCHING

Match the words in Column A with their definitions or descriptions in Column B. Print the letters on the blank lines.

	Column A	Column B
_____	**1.** jog	**A.** a measure of heat
_____	**2.** helmet	**B.** to hit with great force
_____	**3.** license	**C.** very thin
_____	**4.** degree	**D.** to choose by voting
_____	**5.** location	**E.** it protects our head
_____	**6.** skinny	**F.** the best possible
_____	**7.** crazy about	**G.** a place
_____	**8.** perfect	**H.** to run
_____	**9.** crash (into)	**I.** to love very much
_____	**10.** elect	**J.** you need one to drive

3

Celebrations

The Fourth of July

*Reread the dialog "The Fourth of July" (page 47 of **The Salsa Is Hot**) before doing the dialog and word reviews.*

DIALOG REVIEW

*If the sentence is true, write **T**. If it's false, write **F** and change it to a true statement.*

1. _____ The United States celebrates Independence Day on July 4.

   _____

2. _____ The weather report says that it's going to rain.

   _____

3. _____ Gene is going to a parade in the morning.

   _____

4. _____ Karen invites Gene to a cookout.

   _____

5. _____ He can't go to the cookout.

   _____

6. _____ Gene and Karen are going to watch the fireworks on TV.

   _____

7. _____ They're going to listen to music in the park.

   _____

WORD REVIEW

Complete the sentences with these words.

band	cookouts	join	report	swimsuit

1. Karim got all A's and B's on his _____ card. He's happy.

2. In the summer, we have a lot of _____ in our backyard.

3. That's a pretty _____. I'm going to try it on.

4. We're going to play volleyball. Why don't you _____ us?

5. We're having a _____ at our wedding reception.

50

fireworks	sunny	listening	parade	pool

6. I feel better when it's _____.

7. Kelly marched in the _____; she's tired.

8. The workers at the _____ have to be careful.

9. The hotel has an indoor _____.

10. I hope you're _____ to me.

A COUCH POTATO

WORD BANK

To **feel like** is to want to.

A **couch** is another name for a sofa.

A **"couch potato"** is a person who does not get much exercise, who spends a lot of time sitting on a couch watching TV or reading.

Far means at a distance, usually at a long distance.

Around means *about*.

Complete the dialog with these words and practice it with a partner.

boring	feel like	far	couch	join	around	exercise

Dave and Lisa are friends.

Dave: Where are you going?

Lisa: For a walk. Why don't you _____ me?

Dave: Thanks, but I don't _____ going for a walk.

Lisa: You should get more _____.

Dave: I know, but walking is _____.

Lisa: You're getting to be a couch potato.

Dave: I play tennis sometimes.

Lisa: But not very often.

Dave: How _____ do you walk?

Lisa: _____ two miles.

Dave: That's too much for me.

Lisa: What are you going to do?

Dave: Sit on the _____ and watch TV.

WRITING A DIALOG

Work with a partner and create your own dialog. Give your dialog a title.

_____

A: Where are you going?

B: For a walk. Why don't you join me?

A: Thanks, but_____.

B: _____

A: _____

B: _____

A: _____

B: _____

A: _____

SHARING INFORMATION

Discuss these questions with a partner.

1. Do you spend a lot of time watching TV? About how many hours a day?

2. Are you a "couch potato"?

3. Do you ever go for a walk just for exercise? Often?

4. Why is walking very good exercise?

5. Do you think walking is boring? Explain your answer.

6. What other kind of exercise do you do? How often?

7. Many people get their exercise from playing a sport. Do you?

8. Do you feel better after exercising?

Trick or Treat

Reread the dialog "Trick or Treat" (page 50 of **The Salsa Is Hot**) before doing the dialog and word reviews.

DIALOG REVIEW

Answer these questions about the dialog. Use your own ideas to answer the last question.

1. Where is Janet? _____

2. What is she doing? _____

3. Why? _____

4. How do Janet and Matt feel about Halloween? _____

5. What is Greg going to be for Halloween? And Stephanie? _____

6. What are Janet and Matt giving the kids who come to the door? _____

7. Why are they giving the kids money? Give two reasons. _____

   _____

8. Do you think Halloween is a lot of fun? Explain your answer. _____

   _____

WORD REVIEW

Complete the sentences with these words.

astronauts	especially	Halloween	me too	pumpkin

1. _____ is always the last day of October.

2. We're putting a _____ in our window.

3. The United States is proud of its _____.

4. Joe is going to Leslie's party. _____.

5. I like to play tennis, _____ with Kristina.

| pirates | tricks | treat | candle | besides |

6. I'm not going for a walk. I have a headache. _____, it's raining.

7. Sometimes Lee plays _____ on his sister.

8. Put out the _____ before you go to bed.

9. The _____ plan to attack the ship.

10. Going out for dinner is a _____.

HALLOWEEN

The paragraphs below retell the dialog in the form of a story. Complete the paragraphs with these words.

| fun | pirate | besides | Halloween |
| candy | candle | nickels | kids |

Janet is in the kitchen putting a _____ in a pumpkin. She is preparing for _____, which her husband, Matt, thinks is a lot of _____, especially for the _____.

Their son, Greg, is going to be a _____, and their daughter, Stephanie, an astronaut. Janet and Matt are giving the kids who come to the door _____ because they get too much _____. _____, kids love money.

SENTENCE COMPLETION

Complete these sentences.

1. It's fun to _____.

2. Sometimes I _____ too much.

3. I'm not going to the party. I don't feel well. Besides, _____

    _____.

4. Kids love to _____.

5. I love to _____.

6. For Halloween, I want to be a _____.

7. It's a good idea to _____.

8. Kevin _____. "Me too."

WORD GROUPS

Circle the three words that go together.

1. trick or treat   July 4   pumpkin   Halloween
2. jog   swim   water   pool
3. ship   ocean   pirate   police officer
4. parade   picnic   band   march
5. lucky   sunny   cloudy   rainy
6. shirt   swimsuit   hot   shoes

Turkey Day

*Reread the dialog "Turkey Day" (page 53 of **The Salsa Is Hot**) before doing the dialog and word reviews.*

DIALOG REVIEW

*If the sentence is true, write **T**. If it's false, write **F** and change it to a true statement.*

1. _____ Yoko likes Thanksgiving a lot.

   _____

2. _____ She's taking the kids to Macy's to shop.

   _____

3. _____ The kids are happy about going to the parade.

   _____

4. _____ They're afraid of the big balloons.

   _____

5. _____ Sue is going to a football game.

   _____

6. _____ It's the first game of the season.

   _____

7. _____ Sue and Yoko are having the same thing for Thanksgiving dinner.

   _____

WORD REVIEW

Complete the sentences with these words.

excited	together	wonderful	celebrating	team

1. Pablo had a _____ vacation in Peru.
2. Our _____ wasn't very good this year.
3. Abdul and I often have lunch _____.
4. Scott and Eileen are _____ their 20th wedding anniversary.
5. The children are _____ about going to the circus.

balloons	hope	last	season	of course

6. _____, cars are expensive.

7. Our _____ class starts at 1:50 and ends at 2:30.

8. They had a lot of _____ at the party.

9. When does the basketball _____ begin?

10. I _____ I get an A in math.

A BIG PARTY

WORD BANK

When students complete the eighth grade, high school, or college, they
   graduate.
Cheap means costing little.

Complete the dialog with these words and practice it with a partner.

hiring	cheap	excited	wonderful
expensive	graduating	about	

Rich and Dot are friends. Erin is Rich's daughter.

Rich: Erin is _____ from the eighth grade.

Dot: That's _____! Congratulations!

Rich: We're having a big party. I want you to come.

Dot: Of course, I'll come. Where is it?

Rich: We're renting a room in a restaurant.

Dot: That's nice.

Rich: And we're _____ a small band.

Dot: That must be _____.

Rich: Nothing is _____ these days.

Dot: How many people are you having?

Rich: _____ 80.

Dot: Erin must be _____.

Rich: She is. It's a big day for her.

WRITING A DIALOG

Work with a partner and create your own dialog. Give your dialog a title.

_____

A: We're having a big party. I want you to come.

B: _____

A: _____

B: _____

A: _____

B: _____

A: _____

B: _____

DICTATION

1. *Listen while the teacher or your partner reads the dialog without stopping.* **Don't write anything.**
2. *The teacher or your partner will read the dialog a second time, pausing after the missing lines.* **Write in the missing lines.**
3. *The teacher or your partner will read the dialog a third time.* **Check your work.**

Dot: Where's the party?

Rich: _____

Dot: That's nice.

Rich: _____

Dot: That must be expensive.

Rich: _____

Dot: How many people are you having?

Rich: _____

Birthday Presents

Reread the dialog "Birthday Presents" (page 56 of **The Salsa Is Hot**) before doing the dialog and word reviews.

DIALOG REVIEW

Answer these questions about the dialog. Use your own ideas to answer the last question.

1. What is Darryl getting Jason for his birthday? _____

2. How much will it cost? _____

3. How long will it last? _____

4. What does Darryl suggest that Linda give Michelle? _____

5. Why does Linda say no to Darryl's suggestion? _____

    _____

6. What is Darryl's second suggestion? _____

7. What does Linda say about this suggestion? _____

8. Do you think Linda will use the CD player much? Explain your answer. _____

    _____

WORD REVIEW

Complete the sentences with these words.

borrow	earrings	about	last	yet

1. This coat should _____ a long time.

2. I like Debbie's _____. They're different.

3. The store isn't open _____.

4. May I _____ a few chairs for our party?

5. Chen left _____ an hour ago.

suggested	pair	fantastic	once in a while	mind

6. Do you _____ if I join you for lunch?

7. There is a _____ view of the mountains from our hotel.

8. The doctor _____ that I get more sleep.

9. Sal is on a diet, but he eats ice cream _____.

10. I'm going to buy a new _____ of shoes.

A BIKE AND A CD PLAYER

The paragraphs below retell the dialog in the form of a story. Complete the paragraphs with these words.

borrow	earrings	once in a while	about
suggests	fantastic	last	portable

Darryl is getting his son, Jason, a new bike for his birthday. It will cost
_____ $130, and it'll _____ for years. Linda does not know
yet what to get her daughter, Michelle, for her birthday.

Darryl _____ that Linda get her a pair of _____, but
her grandmother is already getting her a pair. Darryl then suggests getting her a
_____ CD player. Linda thinks that is a _____ idea. Darryl
mentions that Linda can _____ the CD player_____.

WORD GROUPS

Circle the three words or phrases that go together.

1. fantastic   great   OK   wonderful

2. bracelet   comb   necklace   earring

3. cousin   friend   brother   grandmother

4. sometimes   once in a while   not often   frequently

5. celebrate   birthday   pie   party

6. balloons   Thanksgiving   November   Thursday

SENTENCE COMPLETION

Complete these sentences.

1. _____ and I _____ together.

2. _____ is a wonderful _____.

3. Sometimes I borrow _____.

4. I don't mind if _____.

5. I _____ once in a while.

6. _____ should last _____.

7. _____ suggested that _____.

8. I didn't _____ yet.

The Pilgrims

Reread the story "The Pilgrims" (page 59 of **The Salsa Is Hot**) before doing the Story Review, Word Review, and Word and Story Review.

STORY REVIEW

If the sentence is true, write **T**. *If it's false, write* **F** *and change it to a true statement.*

1. _____ The Pilgrims came to America from England.

   _____

2. _____ All the people on the *Mayflower* were Pilgrims.

   _____

3. _____ The Pilgrims came to America to make money.

   _____

4. _____ The King of England wouldn't let them worship as they wished.

   _____

5. _____ They landed in Massachusetts in the beginning of the fall.

   _____

6. _____ Many got sick and died.

   _____

7. _____ The Native Americans didn't help the Pilgrims.

   _____

8. _____ The Pilgrims had a big dinner to thank God and their friends.

   _____

WORD REVIEW

Complete the sentences with these words.

decided	own	sailing	go back	getting

1. I have to _____ to the store to return this sweater.
2. Omar has his _____ room.
3. It's four o'clock, and I'm _____ tired.
4. Melissa _____ to buy a new TV.
5. The ship is _____ from California to Mexico.

64

heading	grateful	land	showed	ship

6. Reggie _____ me how to use the computer.

7. I'm very _____ to Reggie.

8. The _____ can carry 1,000 people.

9. The kids are _____ to the park.

10. The plane is going to _____ in Boston.

WORD AND STORY REVIEW

Complete the dialog with these words and practice it with a partner.

land	showed	sailed	plant	got
decide	ship	grateful	worship	Pilgrims

Plymouth, Massachusetts

Mr. Lee is a history teacher, and Sandra is a student.

Mr. Lee: What do you know about the _____ ?

Sandra: They _____ from England to America in 1620.

Mr. Lee: What was the name of their _____ ?

Sandra: That's easy. The *Mayflower*.

Mr. Lee: Why did the Pilgrims come to America?

Sandra: To _____ God in their own way.

Mr. Lee: And where in America did they _____ ?

Sandra: At Plymouth, Massachusetts, in December 1620.

Mr. Lee: What happened to them in Plymouth?

Sandra: Many _____ sick and died.

Mr. Lee: Did the Native Americans help them?

Sandra: Yes, they _____ them how to fish and to _____ corn.

Mr. Lee: Did things get better for the Pilgrims?

Sandra: Yes, by the fall of 1621, they had a lot of food.

Mr. Lee: What did they _____ to do?

Sandra: To have a big dinner to thank God and their Native American friends.
They were very _____ .

Mr. Lee: Very good, Sandra. You know your history.

WRITING

Reread the story of the Pilgrims on page 59 of **The Salsa Is Hot**. *Write a summary of each paragraph in one sentence. (The summary of the first paragraph is done for you.) Then combine the five sentences into a paragraph. The paragraph will be a summary of the story.*

Paragraph 1:   In 1620, the Pilgrims sailed from England to America on the *Mayflower*.
_____

Paragraph 2:   _____
_____

Paragraph 3:   _____
_____

Paragraph 4:   _____
_____

Paragraph 5:   _____
_____

Summary of the Story

_____
_____
_____
_____
_____
_____
_____

On the lines below, list those you are grateful to.

_____   _____   _____

_____   _____   _____

Now write a paragraph telling why you are gratefult to each one. Don't use because *too often.*

Grateful

_____

_____

_____

_____

_____

_____

_____

_____

_____

_____

A Soldier

Reread the dialog "A Soldier" (page 63 of **The Salsa Is Hot**) before doing the dialog and word reviews.

DIALOG REVIEW

If the sentence is true, write **T**. If it's false, write **F** and change it to a true statement.

1. _____ Miles Standish and Squanto are old friends.

   _____

2. _____ Squanto is teaching the Pilgrims how to plant corn.

   _____

3. _____ Miles Standish's job is to defend the Pilgrims.

   _____

4. _____ The *Mayflower* is remaining in Plymouth.

   _____

5. _____ Some Pilgrims are returning to England.

   _____

6. _____ The Pilgrims have great trust in God.

   _____

7. _____ Miles's wife, Rose, is cooking dinner.

   _____

8. _____ Squanto is going to have dinner with Miles.

   _____

WORD REVIEW

Complete the sentences with these words.

courage	pleased	planting	kind	meet

1. Most of my teachers are _____.

2. My parents are _____ with my report card.

3. I want you to _____ my cousin.

4. The soldiers showed great _____ in the war.

5. The farmer is _____ lettuce and carrots.

trust	stayed	hiring	protect	return

6. The bank is _____ more workers.

7. Ryan is going to the post office. He'll _____ in an hour.

8. We _____ in San Francisco for a week.

9. Hockey players have to wear helmets to _____ their heads.

10. I have a very good lawyer. I _____ her.

THE FIRST THANKSGIVING

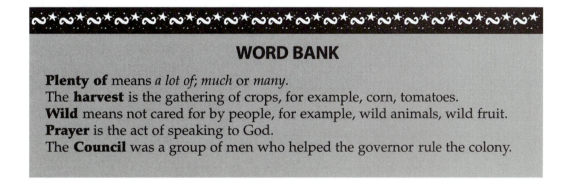

WORD BANK

Plenty of means *a lot of*; *much* or *many*.
The **harvest** is the gathering of crops, for example, corn, tomatoes.
Wild means not cared for by people, for example, wild animals, wild fruit.
Prayer is the act of speaking to God.
The **Council** was a group of men who helped the governor rule the colony.

Complete the dialog with these words and practice it with a partner.

celebration	parade	plenty of	Council	God
wild	difference	prayers	idea	harvest

William Bradford, the governor of Plymouth, is talking to his wife, Dorothy.

William: We have _____ food now.

Dorothy: Yes, we had a great _____.

William: What a _____ from last winter!

Dorothy: True, no one is sick or hungry now.

William: Thank _____!

Dorothy: We should have a big _____.

William: Good _____. We'll celebrate for three days.

Dorothy: The men can shoot some _____ turkeys.

William: And the ladies can prepare a big dinner.

Dorothy: We should invite our Native American friends.

William: Of course. And we can have games.

Dorothy: What do you think of a _____?

William: Fantastic—after we have _____ to thank God.

Dorothy: Miles Standish and his soldiers can lead the parade.

William: Good. I'll speak to the _____ tomorrow.

SHARING INFORMATION

Discuss these questions with a partner.

1. What is the difference between the way the Pilgrims got their turkeys and the way we get turkeys today?

2. The Pilgrims hunted with guns. What did the Native Americans use to hunt? (If you or your partner don't know the name of what they used, ask your teacher or check a bilingual dictionary.)

3. There were no women on the council that helped Governor Bradford rule Plymouth. Why not?

4. Do you think the Pilgrims probably felt they were better than the Native Americans? Explain your answer.

5. Do you think there is still prejudice toward Native Americans in the United States today? Explain your answer.

6. Name some countries, other than the United States, where many Native Americans live today.

7. Do you think there is prejudice toward Native Americans in those countries?

8. We use the adjective *wild* in many different ways. In general, *wild* means "without control." What do you think we mean by a "wild driver" and a "wild idea"?

MATCHING

Match the words in Column A with their definitions or descriptions in Column B.
Print the letters on the blank lines.

	Column A	Column B
_____	1. couch	**A.** to want to
_____	2. around	**B.** to travel by ship
_____	3. feel like	**C.** not cared for by people
_____	4. couch potato	**D.** to consider and choose
_____	5. wild	**E.** speaking to God
_____	6. plenty of	**F.** a sofa
_____	7. sail	**G.** to return
_____	8. prayer	**H.** a lazy person
_____	9. go back	**I.** much or many
_____	10. decide	**J.** about

4

Love

The Big Dance

Reread the dialog "The Big Dance" (page 69 of **The Salsa Is Hot**) before doing the dialog and word reviews.

DIALOG REVIEW

If the sentence is true, write **T**. *If it's false, write* **F** *and change it to a true statement.*

1. _____ Megan is happy.

   _____

2. _____ Dick didn't ask her to go to the big dance.

   _____

3. _____ He's going to the dance with Megan's sister.

   _____

4. _____ Adam thinks Megan is better off without Dick.

   _____

5. _____ She stills loves Dick.

   _____

6. _____ Adam answers the phone.

   _____

7. _____ Megan is going to the dance with Ken.

   _____

WORD REVIEW

Complete the sentences with these words.

fair	calm down	bet	well	cries

1. I _____ that coat costs more than $100.

2. The baby _____ a lot.

3. Mr. and Mrs. Johnson do more for their son than their daughter.

   That's not _____.

4. _____, I don't know what to tell you.

5. Stop shouting and _____. Everything will be OK.

jealous	believe	angry	better off	answered

6. Hakeem phoned his friend, but no one _____.

7. I _____ Gina will help us if we ask her.

8. You would be much _____ with a new car.

9. Sometimes my girlfriend dances with other boys, but I don't get _____.

10. Our boss gets _____ if we're late for work.

OUT FOR THE SEASON

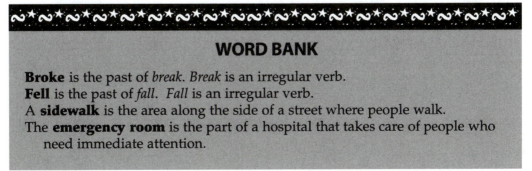

WORD BANK

Broke is the past of *break. Break* is an irregular verb.

Fell is the past of *fall. Fall* is an irregular verb.

A **sidewalk** is the area along the side of a street where people walk.

The **emergency room** is the part of a hospital that takes care of people who need immediate attention.

Complete the dialog with these words and practice it with a partner.

sidewalk	miss	emergency	broke	at least	rest	fell

Laura plays basketball on her high-school team. She is talking to her friend Jesse.

Jesse: Why are you so sad?

Laura: I can't play for the _____ of the season.

Jesse: Why not?

Laura: I _____ my arm.

Jesse: How did that happen?

Laura: I _____ on the ice.

Jesse: When?

Laura: Yesterday. Our _____ was icy.

Jesse: Did they take you to the hospital?

Laura: Yes, to the _____ room of Beth Israel Hospital.

Jesse: How long before you can play?

Laura: _____ four months.

Jesse: The team will _____ you.

Laura: I know. I wish I could play.

WRITING A DIALOG

Work with a partner and create your own dialog. Give your dialog a title.

_____

A: Why are you so sad?

B: I _____.

A: _____

B: _____

A: _____

B: _____

A: _____

B: _____

SHARING INFORMATION

Discuss or complete these statements and questions.

1. Did you ever break a bone?

2. If so, what did you break and how?

3. Did you ever have to go to the emergency room of a hospital? If so, why?

4. How often do you get angry? Often? Sometimes? Rarely? Never?

5. _____ is not fair because _____.

6. Tomorrow I will probably _____.

7. I bet _____.

8. I wish I could _____,

   but I can't because _____.

The Matchmaker

Reread the dialog "The Matchmaker" (page 72 of **The Salsa Is Hot**) before doing the dialog and word reviews.

DIALOG REVIEW

Answer these questions about the dialog. Use your own ideas to answer the last question.

1. How is Kevin's real-estate business doing? _____

2. What did he just sell? _____

3. What does Allison think Kevin is going to be? _____

4. What does she want him to do? _____

5. What does Kevin want to know about Allison's friend? _____

6. What does he have to lose by meeting Allison's friend? _____

7. How does Allison know that Kevin is going to like her friend? _____

_____

8. Do you think Kevin will like Allison's friend? Explain your answer. _____

_____

WORD REVIEW

Complete the sentences with these words.

choice	millionaire	match	just	attractive

1. I'm trying to _____ my brother with a girl who works in my office.

2. Two colleges accepted Leonid. He has to choose one.

   It's a difficult _____.

3. Your girlfriend is very _____.

4. Carolyn makes $100,000 a year, but she's not a _____.

5. The movie _____ started.

by the way	type	matchmaker	real-estate	gain

6. What _____ of job are you looking for?

7. I talked to a _____ agent about selling my house.

8. _____, did you see my keys? I can't find them.

9. You will _____ nothing by fighting with your boss.

10. Brad doesn't have a girlfriend. He needs the help of a _____.

NOTHING TO LOSE

The following paragraphs retell the dialog in the form of a story. Complete the paragraphs with these words.

type	millionaire	choice	match
just	attractive	real-estate	gain

    Kevin is in the _____ business. He _____ sold a

house. His cousin Allison thinks he's going to be a _____ someday, but he

doesn't think so.

    Allison wants to _____ Kevin with a friend of hers. Her friend isn't rich,

but she's _____ and smart.

    Kevin has nothing to lose and everything to _____ by meeting her.

Allison thinks he will like her friend because she's his _____. Kevin didn't like

Allison's last _____, but this one is different.

WORD GROUPS

Circle the three words that go together.

1.	elbow	foot	arm	shoulder
2.	nice	pretty	attractive	beautiful
3.	real estate	house	sidewalk	building
4.	wealthy	boss	millionaire	rich
5.	choose	select	decide	think
6.	sad	unhappy	afraid	sorry

SENTENCE COMPLETION

Complete these sentences. Work with a partner.

1. I believe _____.

2. _____ millionaire.

3. I think _____ is attractive; she's also _____.

4. By the way, _____.

5. Andy just _____.

6. You will gain a lot by _____.

7. You have nothing to lose by _____.

8. Selling houses is _____.

A Lot in Common

Reread the dialog "A Lot in Common" (page 75 of **The Salsa Is Hot**) before doing the dialog and word reviews.

DIALOG REVIEW

If the sentence is true, write **T**. If it's false, write **F** and change it to a true statement.

1. ____ Boris looks great because he's in love.

   _____

2. ____ Anna feels sorry for Nadia.

   _____

3. ____ Boris met Nadia six months ago.

   _____

4. ____ They don't have much in common.

   _____

5. ____ Nadia likes to argue, and she's bossy.

   _____

6. ____ Boris is willing to compromise, but Nadia isn't.

   _____

7. ____ Anna thinks he will be happy.

   _____

WORD REVIEW

Complete the sentences with these words.

bossy	so	argue	lucky	willing

1. Drew never gets headaches. He's _____.

2. Carlos is an excellent soccer player, and _____ is his sister.

3. I'm _____ to help you clean the garage.

4. Marissa likes to _____ with her teachers.

5. My brother is _____, but I don't pay much attention to him.

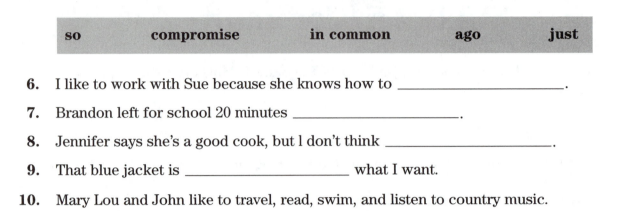

so	compromise	in common	ago	just

6. I like to work with Sue because she knows how to _____.

7. Brandon left for school 20 minutes _____.

8. Jennifer says she's a good cook, but I don't think _____.

9. That blue jacket is _____ what I want.

10. Mary Lou and John like to travel, read, swim, and listen to country music. They have much _____.

ARE YOU TWO IN LOVE?

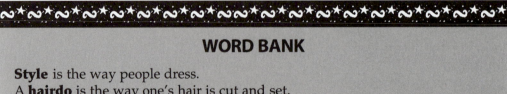

WORD BANK

Style is the way people dress.
A **hairdo** is the way one's hair is cut and set.
An **accountant** is a person who checks financial records.
Handsome means good-looking. *Handsome* is usually said of a man.

Complete the dialog with these words and practice it with a partner.

just	hairdo	too	style
so	wearing	handsome	

Sara is Kate's older sister.

Sara: That's a pretty dress you're _____.

Kate: Thanks. It's not _____ long, is it?

Sara: No, its _____ right. That's the _____ today.

Kate: Do you like my new _____?

Sara: It's great. You must be going somewhere special tonight.

Kate: My boyfriend is taking me to dinner.

Sara: Where did you meet him?

Kate: At work. He's an accountant.

Sara: Is he _____?

Kate: I think _____.

Sara: Are you two in love?

Kate: No, but I like him a lot. He's easy to be with.

WRITING A DIALOG

Work with a partner and create your own dialog. Give your dialog a title.

_____

A: That's a very nice _____ you're wearing.

B: Thanks. I'm going to _____ with _____.

A: _____

B: _____

A: _____

B: _____

A: _____

B: _____

DICTATION

1. *Listen while the teacher or your partner reads the dialog without stopping.* **Don't write anything.**
2. *The teacher or your partner will read the dialog a second time, pausing after the missing lines.* **Write in the missing lines.**
3. *The teacher or your partner will read the dialog a third time.* **Check your work.**

Sara: That's a pretty dress you're wearing.

Kate: _____

Sara: No, it's just right. That's the style today.

Kate: _____

Sara: It's great. You must be going somewhere special tonight.

Kate: _____

Sara: Where did you meet him?

Kate: _____

Valentine's Day

Reread the dialog "Valentine's Day" (page 78 of **The Salsa Is Hot**) before doing the dialog and word reviews.

DIALOG REVIEW

Answer these questions about the dialog. Use your own ideas to answer the last question.

1. What is special about tomorrow? _____

2. Where is Steve taking Jessica? _____

3. What kind of flowers is he getting her? _____

4. What special gift is he getting her? _____

5. How old is Jessica? And Steve? _____

6. Why does Steve say that age doesn't matter? _____

7. What does he say about Joyce? _____

8. Do you see any problem with a 24-year-old man marrying a 32-year-old woman? Explain your answer. _____

WORD REVIEW

Complete the sentences with these words.

favorite	age	so	secret	dozen

1. Jerry got two _____ hamburger rolls for the cookout.

2. "My son got an A in history." "_____? My daughter got an A-plus."

3. I'm wearing my _____ tie to work.

4. & 5. Angela doesn't tell anyone her _____. She wants to keep it a

   _____.

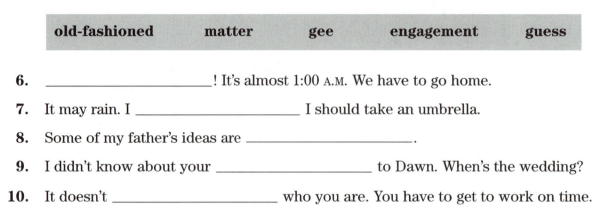

old-fashioned	matter	gee	engagement	guess

6. _____! It's almost 1:00 A.M. We have to go home.

7. It may rain. I _____ I should take an umbrella.

8. Some of my father's ideas are _____.

9. I didn't know about your _____ to Dawn. When's the wedding?

10. It doesn't _____ who you are. You have to get to work on time.

A SPECIAL GIFT

The paragraphs below retell the dialog in the form of a story. Complete the paragraphs with these words.

guesses	secret	old-fashioned	dozen
favorite	matter	Valentine's Day	engagement

Tomorrow is _____. Steve is taking Jessica to their

_____ restaurant. He's also getting her a _____ red roses

and a special gift. He wants to keep the special gift a _____. It is an

_____ ring.

Jessica is 32, and Steve is only 24. Steve's cousin Joyce thinks Steve is too young to marry

Jessica. But Steve believes that age doesn't _____ if you're in love. He thinks

that Joyce is _____. She _____ she is.

WORD GROUPS

Circle the three words or phrases that go together.

1. restaurant   window   food   waitress

2. roses   tulips   grass   flowers

3. young   wedding   engagement   marriage

4. wear   ring   finger   happy

5. So?   Who cares?   gee   not important

6. get   send   obtain   buy

WRITING

In the dialog on page 78 of **The Salsa Is Hot**, Steve says that age doesn't matter if a couple are in love. His cousin Joyce thinks it matters. *What do you think? Write a paragraph of five or six sentences explaining why age matters or why it doesn't matter.*

Note: Your teacher may have two students debate this topic in class.

Hard at First

Reread the story "Hard at First" (page 81 of **The Salsa Is Hot***) before doing the Story Review, Word Review, and Word and Story Review.*

STORY REVIEW

If the sentence is true, write **T**. *If it's false, write* **F** *and change it to a true statement.*

1. _____ Joana came to the United States with her parents and sister.
   _____

2. _____ Her parents worked in a factory when they first came to the United States.
   _____

3. _____ Joana was happy because many of the students were Polish.
   _____

4. _____ At first, she didn't have any friends and was lonely.
   _____

5. _____ She was used to going to a large school.
   _____

6. _____ It took her a long time to make friends and learn English.
   _____

7. _____ She got used to mixing with students from many countries.
   _____

8. _____ She wants very much to become a lawyer.
   _____

WORD REVIEW

Complete the sentences with these words.

get used to	mind (v.)	at first	lonely	dream

1. _____ , my job was very interesting, but now it's boring.

2. Audrey's _____ is to be a pilot.

3. Cory is working from 12 at night to 8 A.M. He has to _____ sleeping during the day.

4. Jean's husband is a sailor. She's _____ when he's at sea.

5. Our teacher doesn't _____ if we talk a little during class.

however	opportunity	such	mixed	noisy

6. The president _____ with the people who came to the dinner.

7. Julio has the _____ to go to a good college.

8. The people leaving the party were very _____ .

9. It's cold out. _____, Roger isn't wearing a coat.

10. It's _____ a beautiful day. We should go to the park.

WORD AND STORY REVIEW

Complete the dialog with these words and practice it with a partner.

lonely	mixed	opportunities	dream	few
understanding	mind	such	noisy	at first

Getting Used to a New School

Edyta is Joana's mother, and Bogdan is a friend of the family.

Bogdan: Why did you come to the United States?

Edyta: So my children would have more _____.

Bogdan: What kind of work did you get?

Edyta: _____, I worked in a factory.

Bogdan: I'm sure that was difficult.

Edyta: Yes, but I didn't _____.

Bogdan: Did Joana like school?

Edyta: In the beginning, she was _____.

Bogdan: I imagine only a _____ students were Polish.

Edyta: That's right, and she wasn't used to _____ a big school.

Bogdan: Were the teachers _____?

Edyta: Most of them were, but she didn't like her lunch period.

Bogdan: Why not?

Edyta: It was too _____.

Bogdan: Did she make new friends at school?

Edyta: Yes, she _____ with students from many countries.

Bogdan: I hear she wants to be a lawyer.

Edyta: That's her _____.

WRITING

A *dream* is something important we very much want to be or to do or to get, for example, to be a teacher, a doctor, a lawyer, to buy a house, to travel to different countries.

Write a composition with the title "My Dream." Write two paragraphs. In the first paragraph, tell all you can about your dream. In the second paragraph, tell what you have to do to make your dream come true.

My Dream

_____

_____

_____

_____

_____

_____

_____

_____

_____

_____

_____

_____

_____

_____

It is clear that it is important for anyone who lives in the United States to learn English.

List as many reasons as you can for learning English, for example, it will help you get a good job.

1. _____

2. _____

3. _____

4. _____

5. _____

6. _____

7. _____

A Diamond Ring

Reread the story "A Diamond Ring" (page 85 of **The Salsa Is Hot**) before doing the Story Review, Word Review, and Word and Story Review.

STORY REVIEW

*If the sentence is true, write **T**. If it's false, write **F** and change it to a true statement.*

1. _____ Joana met Chris at work.
   _____

2. _____ The first time they met, Joana knew she wanted to marry Chris.
   _____

3. _____ They liked to play tennis together.
   _____

4. _____ They took long walks and talked about their jobs, families, and future.
   _____

5. _____ Chris never proposed to Joana because he didn't have to.
   _____

6. _____ He gave her a ring on her 28th birthday.
   _____

7. _____ Joana and Chris are getting married before she graduates from law school.
   _____

8. _____ She isn't lonely anymore.
   _____

WORD REVIEW

Complete the sentences with these words.

chatting	both	diamonds	propose	anymore

1. Larry doesn't jog _____.
2. Of course, _____ are expensive.
3. Ivan and Olga are _____ about their trip to Russia.
4. I want to marry Kathy, but it's too soon to _____ .
5. Beth and Greg have two children, and _____ are good swimmers.

grateful	concert	quickly	joined	no longer

6. Taj shaved _____ and left for work.

7. It's _____ raining.

8. We have an extra ticket for the _____ if you want to go.

9. Danielle _____ the French Club at school.

10. Doug let me borrow his bike. I'm _____.

WORD AND STORY REVIEW

Complete the dialog with these words and practice it with a partner.

both	concerts	miss	diamond	accountant
joined	luck	chatted	proposed	anymore

We Met at the Swim Club

Walter is a friend of Joana.

Walter: Do you still _____ Poland?

Joana: Yes, but since I met Chris, I'm not lonely _____.

Walter: Where did you meet him?

Joana: At the swim club I _____ last summer.

Walter: That's great! Did you see much of him at the club?

Joana: Yes, we played a lot of tennis and _____ about our jobs.

Walter: What does he do?

Joana: He's an _____.

Walter: Does he take you out often?

Joana: Yes. We go to movies, to dinner, and to _____.

Walter: Has he _____ to you?

Joana: Yes, but it wasn't necessary. We _____ knew.

Walter: I see you're wearing a _____ ring.

Joana: Chris gave it to me on my 28th birthday.

Walter: Wonderful! When are you going to get married?

Joana: After I graduate from law school.

Walter: Good _____!

Joana: Thank you.

SENTENCE COMPLETION

Complete these sentences.

1. When I came to the United States, it was hard for me to get used to _____
   _____.

2. I do not _____ anymore.

3. I like to chat with _____.

4. I _____ quickly.

5. At first _____, but now
   _____.

6. It's good to mix with students from other countries because _____
   _____.

7. I'm happy that I have the opportunity to _____
   _____.

8. _____ is noisy.

MATCHING

Match the words in Column A with their definitions or descriptions in Column B.
Print the letters on the blank lines.

Column A	Column B
_____ 1. handsome	**A.** very
_____ 2. style	**B.** from now on
_____ 3. mix	**C.** part of a hospital
_____ 4. such	**D.** to become a member of
_____ 5. at first	**E.** the way people dress
_____ 6. emergency room	**F.** a valuable stone
_____ 7. both	**G.** in the beginning
_____ 8. join	**H.** good-looking
_____ 9. diamond	**I.** the two of them
_____ 10. anymore	**J.** to be with and talk to others

5

Dogs and Money

Man's Best Friend

*Reread the dialog "Man's Best Friend" (page 91 of **The Salsa Is Hot**) before doing the dialog and word reviews.*

DIALOG REVIEW

*If the sentence is true, write **T**. If it's false, write **F** and change it to a true statement.*

1. _____ Nellie is the name of Samir's dog.

   _____

2. _____ Samir doesn't want anyone to touch Nellie.

   _____

3. _____ She barks at people she doesn't know.

   _____

4. _____ She doesn't like Asma.

   _____

5. _____ Nellie is young.

   _____

6. _____ She is always going to be small.

   _____

7. _____ Samir doesn't think Asma should get a dog.

   _____

WORD REVIEW

Complete the sentences with these words.

should	barking	still	licks	pet

1. Is Mrs. Roberts _____ teaching at the high school?

2. We _____ eat more vegetables and fruit.

3. My dog loves it when I _____ her.

4. Why is Spot _____? Is someone at the door?

5. The cat _____ her paws a lot.

biting	other	puppies	stranger	best

6. Tina and I had dinner at the _____ restaurant in town.

7. _____ love to play.

8. Please stop _____ your fingernails.

9. Jack works with me. He isn't a _____.

10. Anish and Vivek are from India. All the _____ students are from Latin America.

A DOG OR A CAT?

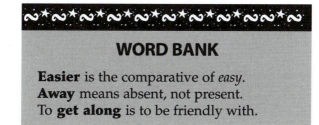

WORD BANK

Easier is the comparative of *easy*.
Away means absent, not present.
To **get along** is to be friendly with.

Complete the dialog with these words and practice it with a partner.

wrong	protect	easier	crazy about
kid	get along	away	

Erin and Nick are married.

Erin: I want to get a cat.

Nick: And I want a dog.

Erin: Cats are much _____ to care for.

Nick: True, but they're not very friendly.

Erin: You're _____ about that.

Nick: How do you know?

Erin: I had a cat when I was a _____.

Nick: A dog will _____ our house. A cat can't.

Erin: But what are we going to do with the dog when we're _____?

Nick: My brother will keep him. He's _____ dogs.

Erin: I have an idea. We can get a dog *and* a cat.

Nick: Great! The dog will be mine and the cat yours.

Erin: I hope they _____.

Nick: Don't worry. They will.

WRITING A DIALOG

Work with a partner and create your own dialog. Give your dialog a title.

_____

A: I want to _____.

B: And I want _____.

A: _____

B: _____

A: _____

B: _____

A: _____

B: _____

SHARING INFORMATION

Discuss these questions with a partner.

1. Some people like dogs but not cats. Some like cats but not dogs. Some like both. Which group are you in?

2. If you had a choice between having a cat or a dog, which would you choose?

3. Why are cats easier to care for?

4. Do you think cats are friendly? Explain your answer.

5. Are most dogs good at protecting their home? Explain your answer.

6. Do you know anyone who has a cat and a dog? If so, how do the cat and dog get along?

7. If you rent an apartment, are you allowed to have a dog? Are you allowed to have a cat?

8. Is there a difference between the way people feel about and care for dogs in your country and in the United States? Answer the same question about cats.

Feeling Lucky

*Reread the dialog "Feeling Lucky" (page 94 of **The Salsa Is Hot**) before doing the dialog and word reviews.*

DIALOG REVIEW

Answer these questions about the dialog. Use your own ideas to answer the last question.

1. Where is Park going? _____

2. How does he feel? _____

3. What does Lee think Park is wasting? _____

4. How much does Park spend on the lottery? _____

5. What is he going to do if he wins? _____

6. Why won't he quit work if he wins? Give two reasons. _____

   _____

7. What can Lee lose by buying a ticket? _____

8. Do you think Lee is going to buy a ticket? Explain your answer.

   _____

   _____

WORD REVIEW

Complete the sentences with these words.

wasted	fun	lottery	retire	win

1. I like to play bingo. It's _____.

2. George is old enough to _____, but he doesn't want to.

3. & 4. The _____ jackpot is up to 10 million. I hope
   I _____.

5. We _____ our time and money going to that movie. It was terrible.

quit	lucky	besides	spend	tickets

6. & 7. Alan is buying ten raffle _____. If he's _____, he'll win a car.

8. Andy and Karen _____ a lot of money on clothes.

9. Heather has a good job, but she's going to _____. She doesn't like her boss.

10. I'm not going swimming today. It's too cold. _____, I'm very tired.

A DOLLAR A WEEK

The paragraphs below retell the dialog in the form of a story. Complete the paragraphs with these words.

wasting	wins	ticket	quit
retire	lucky	besides	spends

Park is going to buy a lottery _____. He feels _____. Lee thinks Park is _____ his time and money. He'll never win.

Park _____ a dollar a week on a ticket. If he _____ the lottery, he's going to buy a house, a car, and a boat, but he won't _____ work. He's too young to _____. _____, he likes his job.

WORD GROUPS

Circle the three words or phrases that go together.

1.	dog	cat	puppy	bark
2.	quit	stop	decide	retire
3.	protect	get along	be friendly	like
4.	nickel	dime	dollar	quarter
5.	spend	use poorly	lose	waste
6.	absent	sick	not here	away

SHARING INFORMATION

Discuss or complete these statements and questions.

1. What do you think is a good age to retire? Explain your answer.

2. Do you think most people who retire find enough to do and are happy? Or do you think most find their retirement boring? Explain your answer.

3. Some people who win the lottery spend their money foolishly and would be better off if they never had won. What do you think lottery winners should do with their money?

4. I spend a lot of time _____.

5. I think I should spend more time _____.

6. I waste time _____.

7. Do you think you waste money? If so, how?

8. Name some things people waste besides time and money.

A Big Shot

Reread the dialog "A Big Shot" (page 97 of **The Salsa Is Hot***) before doing the story and word reviews.*

STORY REVIEW

If the sentence is true, write **T**. *If it's false, write* **F** *and change it to a true statement.*

1. _____ Diana is very unhappy.

   _____

2. _____ She never fights with her husband.

   _____

3. _____ She is complaining about his spending.

   _____

4. _____ Wayne thinks she spends too much.

   _____

5. _____ She admits she's cheap.

   _____

6. _____ She likes to save money.

   _____

7. _____ She doesn't think they have enough money for what Wayne wants.

   _____

WORD REVIEW

Complete the sentences with these words.

cheap	afford	fancy	matter	complains

1. I don't know what's the _____ with my car, but it won't start.

2. We looked at a nice house in a quiet neighborhood. I hope we can
   _____ it.

3. Mrs. Walters _____ that her husband never helps with the housework.

4. & 5. My boyfriend took me to a _____ restaurant.
   He isn't _____.

argue	sense	upset	argument	big shot

6. Barbara's son drinks too much. She's very _____.

7. Kyle likes to _____ with his parents.

8. My boss thinks he's a _____.

9. Dr. Stevens tells his patients not to smoke, but he smokes himself. That doesn't make
_____.

10. I got into an _____ with my daughter about one of her friends.

UP UNTIL 2 A.M.

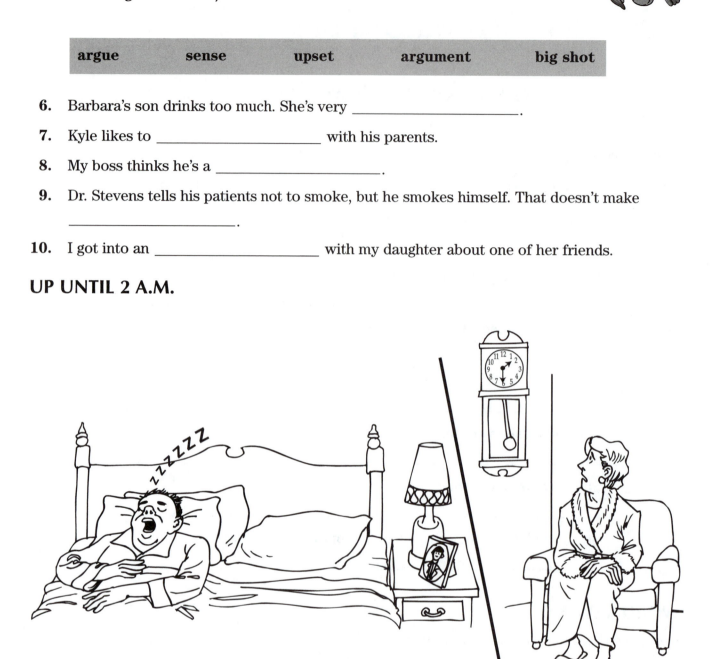

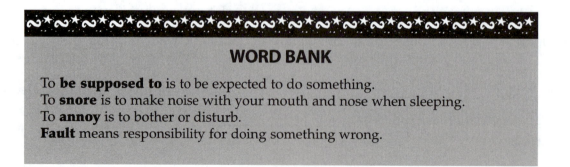

WORD BANK

To **be supposed to** is to be expected to do something.
To **snore** is to make noise with your mouth and nose when sleeping.
To **annoy** is to bother or disturb.
Fault means responsibility for doing something wrong.

Complete the dialog with these words and practice it with a partner.

annoys	around	bit	supposed
snoring	fault	concert	

Justin and Ashley are friends. Paul is Ashley's son, and he's 17 years old.

Justin: You look tired.

Ashley: I am. I was up until two A.M. waiting for Paul.

Justin: Where was he?

Ashley: At a _____ with two of his friends.

Justin: What time was he _____ to be home?

Ashley: _____ one-thirty, but the concert started late.

Justin: Where was your husband?

Ashley: He was in bed _____ .

Justin: Doesn't he worry when Paul is late?

Ashley: Not one _____ , and that _____ me.

Justin: But it's not his _____ that you worry so much.

Ashley: No, but he could stay up with me.

Justin: Did Paul drive to the concert?

Ashley: Yes, and that's what worried me most.

WRITING A DIALOG

Work with a partner and create your own dialog. Give your dialog a title.

_____

A: You look upset. What's the matter?

B: _____

A: _____

B: _____

A: _____

B: _____

A: _____

B: _____

DICTATION

1. Listen while the teacher or your partner reads the dialog without stopping. **Don't write anything.**
2. The teacher or your partner will read the dialog a second time, pausing after the missing lines. **Write in the missing lines.**
3. The teacher or your partner will read the dialog a third time. **Check your work.**

Justin: You look tired.

Ashley: _____

Justin: Where was he?

Ashley: _____

Justin: What time was he supposed to be home?

Ashley: _____

Justin: Where was your husband?

Ashley: _____

New Furniture

Reread the dialog "New Furniture" (page 100 of **The Salsa Is Hot**) before doing the dialog and word reviews.

DIALOG REVIEW

Answer these questions about the dialog. Use your own ideas to answer the last question.

1. Where does Jim want to go with his wife? _____

2. What does she want to do first? _____

3. For what? _____

4. What did Pat and Jim just get for the living room? _____

5. What doesn't Jim understand? _____

6. What doesn't match? _____

7. What will Pat and Jim have time for if they leave now? _____

8. Do you think that Pat's friends would notice if the rug and the furniture didn't match? Explain your answer. _____

_____

WORD REVIEW

Complete the sentences with these words.

honey	match	let's	noticed	rug

1. The dog is lying on the _____.

2. _____ listen to some music and relax.

3. How do you like my new dress, _____?

4. I _____ that Sandra has a new car.

5. Your shirt and pants don't _____.

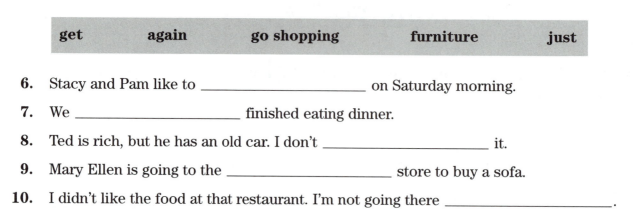

| get | again | go shopping | furniture | just |

6. Stacy and Pam like to _____ on Saturday morning.

7. We _____ finished eating dinner.

8. Ted is rich, but he has an old car. I don't _____ it.

9. Mary Ellen is going to the _____ store to buy a sofa.

10. I didn't like the food at that restaurant. I'm not going there _____.

NO MONEY

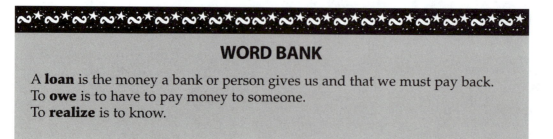

WORD BANK

A **loan** is the money a bank or person gives us and that we must pay back.
To **owe** is to have to pay money to someone.
To **realize** is to know.

Complete the dialog with these words and practice it with a partner.

borrow	realize	expensive	loan
guess	hire	owe	

Terry and Alex are married.

Terry: I think we should paint our living room and kitchen.

Alex: That's a nice idea, but I can't paint.

Terry: I know, but we can _____ a painter.

Alex: That'll be _____, and we don't have the money.

Terry: We can _____ the money from the bank.

Alex: But we already have a car _____.

Terry: How much do we _____ on it?

Alex: About $10,000.

Terry: Wow! I didn't _____ that.

Alex: Maybe we can paint next year.

Terry: Yes, I _____ we'll have to wait.

WORD GROUPS

Circle the three words that go together.

1. living room   kitchen   basement   dining room

2. chair   window   table   furniture

3. notice   see   look at   imagine

4. trick   annoy   bother   disturb

5. worried   tired   upset   unhappy

6. realize   know   understand   guess

SHARING INFORMATION

Discuss or complete these statements and questions.

1. I would like to _____, but I can't afford it.

2. Sometimes I complain about _____.

3. Name something that annoys you.

4. Do you ever go to concerts? If so, how often and where?

5. When do you usually go shopping?

6. How often do you go to the movies? Do you ever go to a movie in your first language? If so, where?

7. Let's _____.

8. Did you ever borrow money from a bank? If so, what for?

Very Different

Reread the story "Very Different" (page 103 of **The Salsa Is Hot**) before doing the Story Review, Word Review, and Word and Story Review.

STORY REVIEW

If the sentence is true, write **T**. *If it's false, write* **F** *and change it to a true statement.*

1. ____ Tim doesn't say much and doesn't laugh a lot.
   _____

2. ____ Nancy is quiet.
   _____

3. ____ She's short and thin.
   _____

4. ____ Tim eats hamburgers.
   _____

5. ____ Nancy likes to shop and doesn't worry about the cost of things.
   _____

6. ____ Tim loves to save money.
   _____

7. ____ He likes to watch the news, and in the fall he watches basketball.
   _____

8. ____ Nancy likes to watch movies, but she doesn't think the news is interesting.
   _____

WORD REVIEW

Complete the sentences with these words.

jokes	even	so	overweight	laugh

1. Shawn goes for a walk _____ when it's very cold.

2. Donna has lost 20 pounds, but she's still _____.

3. & 4. Our teacher likes to tell _____, and I _____ at most of them.

5. Trevor was tired, _____ he went to bed early.

111

whatever	mall	although	news	prefers

6. I listen to the _____ when I drive to work.

7. On Labor Day, all the stores at the _____ have big sales.

8. Amanda is a good soccer player, but she _____ to play tennis.

9. _____ Vince is thin, he's very strong.

10. In the army, you have to do _____ you're told.

WORD AND STORY REVIEW

Complete the dialog with these words and practice it with a partner.

prefers	news	overweight	although	malls
even	so	whatever	vegetarian	jokes

Nancy Likes to Shop; Tim Likes to Save

Lauren and Ben are friends. Ben is Nancy's cousin.

Lauren: You must know Tim and Nancy well.

Ben: I do. And _____ they're happy, they're very different.

Lauren: So I've noticed. He's serious and never tells _____.

Ben: She can make anyone laugh, _____ Tim.

Lauren: He's tall and thin.

Ben: She's short and a little _____.

Lauren: He's a _____, _____ he never eats meat.

Ben: She eats anything you put in front of her.

Lauren: She likes to go to parties.

Ben: He _____ to stay home and read.

Lauren: She likes to shop at the _____ and buys _____ she wants.

Ben: He likes to save and go to the bank.

Lauren: She watches movies and talk shows on TV.

Ben: He watches the _____.

WRITING

Write a composition about two people—two friends, two brothers, two sisters, a brother and a sister, a married couple. The two get along very well, but they are also very different. Describe how they are different. Write three paragraphs. They can be short. Do not copy from the story on page 103 of **The Salsa Is Hot***, but imitate the story in a general way. You can work with a partner or by yourself.*

_____

_____

_____

_____

_____

_____

_____

_____

_____

_____

_____

_____

_____

_____

_____

_____

Write one paragraph describing the ways in which you and your best friend are the same (what you have in common) and how you are different.

_____

_____

_____

_____

_____

_____

_____

Mark, Emily, and Midnight

Reread the story "Mark, Emily, and Midnight" (page 107 of **The Salsa Is Hot**) before doing the Story Review, Word Review, and Word and Story Review.

STORY REVIEW

If the sentence is true, write **T**. *If it's false, write* **F** *and change it to a true statement.*

1. _____ Tim worries about Mark and Emily more than Nancy does.
   _____

2. _____ Nancy checks carefully where Mark and Emily are going and who they're with.
   _____

3. _____ Mark has to be home by 11:30 or 12:00.
   _____

4. _____ Mark is a very good soccer player, but Emily doesn't play sports.
   _____

5. _____ Nancy talks a lot to the other parents at Mark and Emily's games.
   _____

6. _____ Nancy and Tim like dogs.
   _____

7. _____ Tim doesn't complain about Midnight since Nancy takes care of him.
   _____

8. _____ Midnight jumps up on Tim when he comes home.
   _____

WORD REVIEW

Complete the sentences with these words.

concentrate	insists	checks	feed	close

1. Tyler _____ on his tomato plants every day.
2. The nurse keeps a _____ watch on the patients.
3. _____ on what you're doing and forget everything else.
4. Visitors at the zoo aren't supposed to _____ the animals.
5. When the teacher is talking, she _____ on silence.

114

objected	jump	tails	at all	since

6. The children like to _____ on the bed.

7. Ahmad just came to the United States. He doesn't speak English _____.

8. Brenda's parents _____ to her marriage to Victor.

9. I turned on the air-conditioning _____ it was so hot.

10. Monkeys have long _____.

WORD AND STORY REVIEW

Complete the dialog with these words and practice it with a partner.

feeds	both	concentrates	jumps	insists
at all	wag	check	chats	object

Two Teenagers and a Dog

Lauren and Ben are friends. Ben is Nancy's cousin.

Lauren: Are Tim and Nancy's children teenagers?

Ben: Yes, and that's why Nancy keeps a close _____ on them.

Lauren: Do they have to be in by a certain time?

Ben: Nancy _____ that Mark be home by 11:30 or 12:00.

Lauren: Is Emily still playing basketball and Mark, soccer?

Ben: Yes, and _____ Tim and Nancy go to all their games.

Lauren: I bet Nancy _____ a lot with the other parents.

Ben: Of course, and Tim _____ on the games.

Lauren: Does Nancy still have Midnight?

Ben: Yes, she loves dogs, but Tim doesn't like them _____.

Lauren: Does he _____ to Nancy having a dog?

Ben: Why should he? She walks, _____, and takes care of Midnight.

Lauren: Midnight must love her.

Ben: He does. When she comes home, he _____ up on her and licks her hands.

Lauren: What does he do when Tim comes home?

Ben: Nothing. He doesn't even get up or _____ his tail.

ADDING *-ION* TO VERBS

English often adds *-ion* to a verb to form a noun. For example, we add *-ion* to the verb *concentrate* to form the noun *concentration*. (Note that we drop the final *e* in *concentrate* before adding *-ion*.). *Concentration* is the act of *concentrating*. Below are some verbs used in **The Salsa Is Hot** that form a noun by adding *-ion*.

Verbs	Nouns
imagine	imagination
object	objection
protect	protection
suggest	suggestion
decide	decision

Complete these sentences.

objection	suggestion	imagination	decision	protection

1. Our eyes need _____ from the sun. That's why we should wear sunglasses.

2. To write a story, you have to use your _____.

3. I asked to use my father's car, and he had no _____.

4. Alex quit school. I think he made a bad _____.

5. Do you mind if I make a _____?

MATCHING

Match the words in Column A with their definitions or descriptions in Column B. Print the letters on the blank lines.

Column A	Column B
_____ 1. get along	**A.** to bother
_____ 2. away	**B.** for that reason
_____ 3. realize	**C.** surprisingly
_____ 4. annoy	**D.** to have to pay
_____ 5. even	**E.** to make noise when sleeping
_____ 6. prefer	**F.** absent; not present
_____ 7. owe	**G.** should
_____ 8. so	**H.** to be friendly with
_____ 9. snore	**I.** to like better
_____ 10. be supposed to	**J.** to know

6

Food

I'm Starving

Reread the dialog "I'm Starving" (page 113 of **The Salsa Is Hot**) before doing the dialog and word reviews.

DIALOG REVIEW

*If the sentence is true, write **T**. If it's false, write **F** and change it to a true statement.*

1. _____ Carol is in the living room.

   _____

2. _____ She's talking on the telephone.

   _____

3. _____ Nick is cooking dinner.

   _____

4. _____ Ryan is in the kitchen.

   _____

5. _____ He's fixing his bike.

   _____

6. _____ Nick is very hungry.

   _____

7. _____ He never eats meat.

   _____

WORD REVIEW

Complete the sentences with these words.

fixing	getting	disturb	great	basement

1. You'll need a coat. It's _____ cold.

2. We had a _____ vacation. We went to Canada.

3. Adam is _____ our front door.

4. We have a big problem. It's raining, and there's water in our _____.

5. The principal is talking to some parents. Don't _____ them.

relaxing	favorite	hates	starving	bike

6. Evan is listening to music and _____.

7. May I borrow your _____ for an hour?

8. "I Love You So" is Monica's _____ song.

9. We can't wait to eat. We're _____.

10. Rachel _____ to shop for food.

COACHES AND PARENTS

WORD BANK

To **yell (at)** is to shout—to speak in a very loud voice.

Patience is the ability to accept calmly what one doesn't like.

In baseball, the **umpire** stands behind the catcher and calls "balls" and "strikes." Look at the drawing on page 36 of **The Salsa Is Hot**.

Really means *very*.

To **boo** is to shout "boo" to show you don't like a person or what a person is doing.

Complete the dialog with these words and practice it with a partner.

patience	boo	yells	really
polite	coach	argues	

Ricardo and Michelle are parents and friends.

Ricardo: Is your son playing baseball this year?

Michelle: Yes, he's playing in Little League.

Ricardo: What do you know about his _____?

Michelle: He's very good. He never _____ at the kids.

Ricardo: He must have a lot of _____.

Michelle: He does, but sometimes he _____ with the umpires.

Ricardo: That's OK. Many coaches do. How do the parents act?

Michelle: Most are fine, but a few are _____ bad.

Ricardo: What do you mean?

Michelle: They shout at the umpire. They _____ the other team.

Ricardo: That's terrible.

Michelle: I know. They want their kids to be _____, but they aren't.

WRITING A DIALOG

Work with a partner and create your own dialog. Give your dialog a title.

_____

A: Are you cooking dinner tonight? _____

B: No, _____.

A: _____

B: _____

A: _____

B: _____

A: _____

B: _____

SHARING INFORMATION

Discuss these questions with a partner.

1. All teams have a coach. How important is the coach? Explain your answer.

2. Coaches often yell at their players. Why? Is that OK?

3. Does the yelling help? Explain your answer.

4. Do coaches need a lot of patience? Explain your answer.

5. Does it help to argue with umpires? Explain your answer.

6. Do you think a baseball umpire has a tough job? Explain your answer.

7. Do you think many parents take their children's games too seriously? Explain your answer.

8. In sports, do you think too much emphasis is put on winning and not enough on having fun and doing your best? Explain your answer.

More Chicken!

Reread the dialog "More Chicken!" *(page 116 of* **The Salsa Is Hot**) *before doing the dialog and word reviews.*

DIALOG REVIEW

Answer these questions about the dialog. Use your own ideas to answer the last question.

1. Why does Sara cook chicken so often? Give two reasons. _____

   _____

2. Why doesn't Pete want chicken? _____

3. How does Sara feel about cooking? _____

4. What suggestion does she make to Pete? _____

5. What is his reply? _____

6. What does she tell him to do if he's not going to cook? _____

   _____

7. How does Pete feel? _____

8. Do you think he will ever learn how to cook? Explain your answer. _____

   _____

WORD REVIEW

Complete the sentences with these words.

maybe	tired of	then	argue	nonsense

1. I'm _____ this cold weather. I want to move to Los Angeles.

2. Dustin has some good ideas, but a lot of what he says is _____ .

3. My cousin is leaving the hospital today. _____ he must be getting better.

4. _____ I'll go fishing tomorrow.

5. You can _____ with Brittany all day, but she won't change.

complain	let's	probably	mood	so

6. The test was _____ long I couldn't finish it.

7. I will _____ see Cynthia this afternoon.

8. The workers _____ that the boss is always checking on them.

9. This rain doesn't help my _____.

10. I'm hungry. _____ order a pizza.

MAYBE PETE SHOULD COOK

The paragraphs below retell the dialog in the form of a story. Complete the paragraphs with these words.

tired of	complaining	nonsense	mood
argue	besides	probably	so

Sara is cooking chicken for dinner. Her husband, Pete, asks her why they have _____ much chicken. She tells him it's because she likes chicken. _____, it's easy to cook. Pete is _____ chicken.

Sara suggests that maybe Pete should cook. He says he can't. Sara thinks that's _____. A lot of men cook today.

Pete tells his wife he doesn't want to _____. So Sara asks him about his job. He had a terrible day at work, and he's in a bad _____.

Maybe that's why he's _____ about the chicken, Sara says. He says that's _____ true.

WORD GROUPS

Circle the three words or phrases that go together.

1. possibly　　probably　　clearly　　maybe

2. boo　　kid (v.)　　complain　　object (v.)

3. yell　　shout　　speak　　argue

4. boat　　car　　bike　　motorcycle

5. relax　　laugh　　rest　　take it easy

6. please　　of course　　polite　　thank you

SHARING INFORMATION

Discuss or complete these statements and questions.

1. I'm tired of _____.

2. Tomorrow I'll probably _____.

3. Tell something that people do that you think is nonsense—that doesn't make sense.

4. What kind of mood are you in now? Are you usually in a good mood?

5. Name a food you eat a lot. Are you tired of it?

6. If you eat at school, what do you think of the food in your school cafeteria?

7. Is it easy to cook, or is cooking hard work? Explain your answer.

8. Do you think cooking is boring or interesting? Explain your answer.

The Salsa Is Hot

Reread the dialog "The Salsa Is Hot" (page 119 of **The Salsa Is Hot**) before doing the dialog and word reviews.

DIALOG REVIEW

*If the sentence is true, write **T**. If it's false, write **F** and change it to a true statement.*

1. _____ Paul is hungry, but Erica isn't.

   _____

2. _____ She wants to stop at McDonald's.

   _____

3. _____ Paul didn't have lunch.

   _____

4. _____ He likes Mexican food.

   _____

5. _____ Erica is getting nachos and a salad.

   _____

6. _____ Paul likes spicy food.

   _____

7. _____ Erica doesn't mind spicy food.

   _____

WORD REVIEW

Complete the sentences with these words.

so	how about	tacos	warned	spicy

1. Diego likes hamburgers, but he prefers _____.

2. Chelsea loves country music, and _____ do I.

3. I can't eat this chili con carne. It's too _____.

4. _____ going for a swim in our pool?

5. Jesse _____ me that this restaurant is expensive.

125

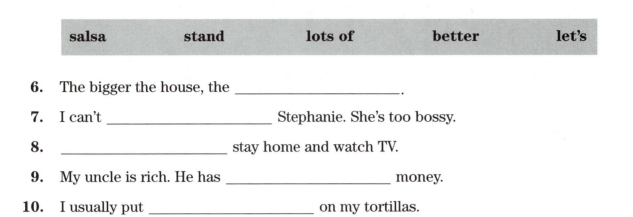

salsa	stand	lots of	better	let's

6. The bigger the house, the _____.

7. I can't _____ Stephanie. She's too bossy.

8. _____ stay home and watch TV.

9. My uncle is rich. He has _____ money.

10. I usually put _____ on my tortillas.

A GREAT COOK

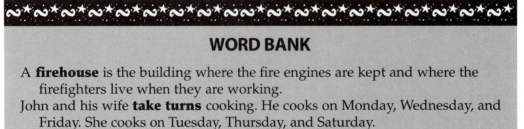

WORD BANK

A **firehouse** is the building where the fire engines are kept and where the firefighters live when they are working.

John and his wife **take turns** cooking. He cooks on Monday, Wednesday, and Friday. She cooks on Tuesday, Thursday, and Saturday.

A **meal** is the food you eat at breakfast, lunch, or dinner.

Complete the dialog with these words and practice it with a partner.

firehouse	better than	lucky	baked
meal	fantastic	take turns	

Mario and Kelly work for the same company.

Mario: Who cooks in your family?

Kelly: My husband, Ed. He's a _____ cook.

Mario: You're _____. Where did he learn?

Kelly: At the _____. He's a firefighter.

Mario: That's great!

Kelly: The firefighters _____ cooking.

Mario: Do they all cook?

Kelly: Yes, but some are _____ others.

Mario: Do you ever cook?

Kelly: Only when Ed is at the firehouse.

Mario: What's Ed's best _____?

Kelly: _____ ziti. The next time he cooks it, I'll invite you to dinner.

Mario: Why, thank you.

WRITING A DIALOG

Work with a partner and create your own dialog. Give your dialog a title.

_____

A: My husband is a fantastic cook.

B: _____

A: _____

B: _____

A: _____

B: _____

A: _____

B: _____

DICTATION

1. *Listen while the teacher or your partner reads the dialog without stopping.* **Don't write anything.**
2. *The teacher or your partner will read the dialog a second time, pausing after the missing lines.* **Write in the missing lines.**
3. *The teacher or your partner will read the dialog a third time.* **Check your work.**

Mario: Who cooks in your family?

Kelly: _____

Mario: You're lucky. Where did he learn?

Kelly: _____

Mario: That's great!

Kelly: _____

Mario: Do they all cook?

Kelly: _____

The C.I.A.

*Reread the dialog "The C.I.A." (page 122 of **The Salsa Is Hot**) before doing the dialog and word reviews.*

DIALOG REVIEW

Answer these questions about the dialog. Use your own ideas to answer the last question.

1. What is the C.I.A.? Name two possibilities. _____

    _____

2. What does Lisa think Gary is going to do? _____

3. Why is he going to the C.I.A.? _____

4. Is the C.I.A. a good school? _____

5. How do they train you to be a chef? _____

6. Who do the students at the C.I.A. cook for? _____

7. Who can eat at the C.I.A.'s restaurant? _____

8. Do you think a graduate of the C.I.A. can easily get a job as a chef? Explain your answer.

    _____

WORD REVIEW

Complete the sentences with these words.

graduate	best	spies	cheap	have got to

1. Soup is _____.

2. Duke is one of the _____ universities in the United States.

3. We _____ clean the basement.

4. In the Cold War, both the United States and the Soviet Union used _____.

5. What are you going to do after you _____ from high school?

.

129

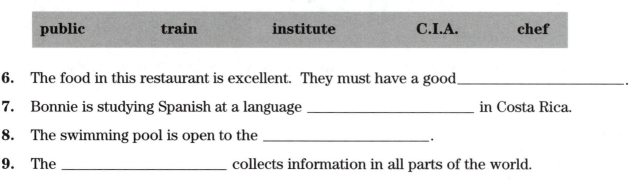

public	train	institute	C.I.A.	chef

6.   The food in this restaurant is excellent. They must have a good_____.

7.   Bonnie is studying Spanish at a language _____ in Costa Rica.

8.   The swimming pool is open to the _____.

9.   The _____ collects information in all parts of the world.

10. The army has camps to _____ soldiers.

A LAND OF INITIALS

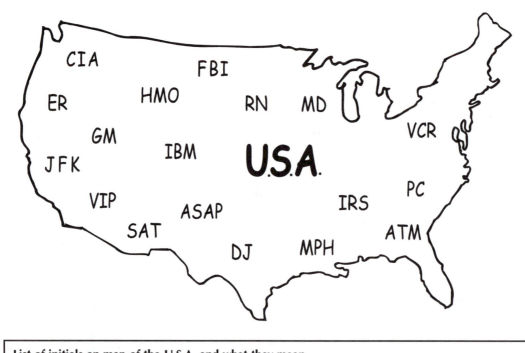

List of initials on map of the U.S.A. and what they mean

ER	= emergency room		VIP	= very important person
HMO	= health maintenance organization		ASAP	= as soon as possible
RN	= registered nurse		PC	= personal computer
MD	= medical doctor		DJ	= disc jockey
GM	= General Motors		MPH	= miles per hour
IBM	= International Business Machines		ATM	= automated teller machine
VCR	= video cassette recorder		CIA	= Central Intelligence Agency
SAT	= Scholastic Aptitude Test		IRS	= Internal Revenue Service

WORD BANK

Initials are the first letters of the name of a person or thing. For example, JFK are the initials of John F. Kennedy and of the airport named after him, ER of the emergency room, and FBI of the Federal Bureau of Investigation.

To **require** is to say that something is necessary.

Complete the dialog with these words and practice it with a partner.

applying	initials	join	require
of course	rough	plenty	

Miguel and Paula are friends.

Miguel: The United States is a country of _____.

Paula: What do you mean?

Miguel: We have the FBI, the ER, JFK, and _____ the U.S.A.

Paula: And I bet there are _____ more.

Miguel: Definitely. I'm _____ to college, and I have to take the SAT.

Paula: What's that?

Miguel: The Scholastic Aptitude Test. Most colleges _____ it.

Paula: It sounds _____.

Miguel: It is. It tests how much math and English you know.

Paula: And I have a friend who wants to _____ the NYPD.

Miguel: The what?

Paula: The New York Police Department.

Miguel: You see, we live in a land of initials.

WORD GROUPS

Circle the three words that go together.

1.	too	also	yet	so
2.	spy	apply	C.I.A.	secret
3.	supermarket	chef	cook	restaurant
4.	firefighter	police officer	secretary	letter carrier
5.	spaghetti	potatoes	ziti	pizza
6.	culinary	food	kitchen	table

SHARING INFORMATION

Discuss or complete these statements and questions.

1. Name some fast-food restaurants besides Taco Bell and McDonald's.

2. Are hamburgers popular in your country? Do you like hamburgers?

3. I can't stand _____.

4. I warned _____.

5. Who cooks in your family?

6. _____ is cheap.

7. Give an example of initials (ones not used in this chapter) commonly used in the United States.

8. Is the use of initials as common in your first language as in English? If so, give an example.

A Store and a Home

Reread the story "A Store and a Home" (page 125 of **The Salsa Is Hot**) before doing the Story Review, Word Review, and Word and Story Review.

STORY REVIEW

*If the sentence is true, write **T**. If it's false, write **F** and change it to a true statement.*

1. _____ Kala and Ankita Patel speak Gujarati.

   _____

2. _____ Kala's first job was in a grocery store.

   _____

3. _____ Ankita worked as a waitress in an Indian restaurant.

   _____

4. _____ Now they run a small grocery store.

   _____

5. _____ Their store is open 18 hours a day.

   _____

6. _____ They take a week's vacation every year.

   _____

7. _____ Last year they bought a house, their big goal.

   _____

8. _____ Their house is large and pretty.

   _____

WORD REVIEW

Complete the sentences with these words.

languages	groceries	hurry	neighborhood	midnight

1. Katie left her house in a _____. She didn't want to be late for work.

2. Joshua works from four in the afternoon until _____.

3. I put the _____ on the kitchen table.

4. The people in our _____ are very friendly.

5. They teach many _____ in our high school—Spanish, French, Italian, Latin, German, and Russian.

133

goal	vacation	earn	either	sacrifies

6. We're going to Spain for our _____.

7. Vanessa made many _____ to become a tennis star.

8. Ron is a social worker. He doesn't _____ a lot, but he likes his job.

9. Francisco's_____ is to save enough money to buy a new car.

10. I'm going to get _____ a hamburger or a hot dog.

WORD AND STORY REVIEW

Complete the dialog with these words and practice it with a partner.

proud	groceries	sacrifices	grocery store	neighborhood
earn	goal	language	vacation	midnight

Long Hours

Kenji and Mitra study English at a night school. They are friends and are talking about Ankita during a break.

Kenji: English is a difficult _____, isn't it?

Mitra: Very.

Kenji: Do you know Ankita well?

Mitra: She's my cousin. She worked in the _____ I own.

Kenji: Where does she work now?

Mitra: Ankita and her husband have their own store.

Kenji: What do they sell?

Mitra: Newspapers, milk, bread, and other _____.

Kenji: I'm sure they work long hours.

Mitra: From six in the morning until _____.

Kenji: Do you think they _____ much?

Mitra: Yes, but they make many _____.

Kenji: When do they go on _____?

Mitra: They don't.

Kenji: Did they get a house yet?

Mitra: Yes, they just bought a pretty house in a quiet _____.

Kenji: I'm sure they're _____ of it.

Mitra: Of course. Buying a house was their big _____.

WRITING

Write a story about a person or a couple who come to the United States from your country. At first the person (or couple) works for someone else and gains experience. Then they (or he or she) run their own business—any business you wish to write about. For example, at first the newcomer works as a painter for someone else. Then he (or she) opens up his own business painting houses. Imitate the story of Kala and Ankita in a general way.

_____

_____

_____

_____

_____

_____

_____

_____

_____

_____

_____

_____

_____

_____

Complete one of these sentences.

1. Someday I want to have my own business because _____

_____

2. I don't want to have my own business because _____

_____

Growing Up in America

Reread the story "Growing Up in America" (page 129 of **The Salsa Is Hot**) before doing the Story Review, Word Review, and Word and Story Review.

STORY REVIEW

If the sentence is true, write **T**. *If it's false, write* **F** *and change it to a true statement.*

1. _____ Jay is going to study computer science in college.

   _____

2. _____ Sports aren't very important to him.

   _____

3. _____ He works at the convenience store after school.

   _____

4. _____ His family understands the value of education.

   _____

5. _____ Manda is a very good student and especially likes biology and history.

   _____

6. _____ She wants to be a doctor so she can make a lot of money.

   _____

7. _____ She's a good swimmer and wants to be a lifeguard.

   _____

8. _____ After school on Thursday, she takes singing lessons.

   _____

WORD REVIEW

Complete the sentences with these words.

engineering	interfere	seniors	however	importance

1. The trees _____ with our view.
2. Ricky is a good student. _____, he got 50 on his math test.
3. Stevens Institute of Technology has a good _____ program.
4. The English teachers are discussing the _____ of grammar.
5. There are four _____ on the basketball team.

lifeguards	emphasizes	grade	pediatrician	so

6. The _____ is examining my son.

7. Our football coach_____ defense.

8. Sharon is going to the library _____ she can study.

9. Mrs. Suarez teaches the fourth _____.

10. Phil is applying to a program that trains _____.

WORD AND STORY REVIEW

Complete the dialog with these words and practice it with a partner.

engineering	bother	interfere	enough	pediatrician
importance	senior	lifeguard	emphasize	grade

Doing Well in School

Ravi meets Ankita at a party.

Ravi: How many children do you have?

Ankita: Two—Jayesh and Manda.

Ravi: Are they old _____ to go to school?

Ankita: Yes, Manda is in the seventh _____; Jay is a _____ in high school.

Ravi: Is Jay going to college next year?

Ankita: Yes, he's going to study _____.

Ravi: Does he work after school?

Ankita: No, we don't want anything to _____ with his schoolwork.

Ravi: I can see that you _____ education.

Ankita: Yes, and Jay and Manda understand the _____ of doing well in school.

Ravi: What does Manda want to be?

Ankita: She wants to be a _____ so she can help children.

Ravi: She will have to study hard.

Ankita: That won't _____ her—she likes to study.

Ravi: Does she like sports?

Ankita: She likes to play volleyball and to swim.

Ravi: Is she a good swimmer?

Ankita: Yes, very good. Someday she hopes to be a _____.

SHARING INFORMATION

Discuss or complete these statements and questions.

1. Is there a convenience store near your home? If so, when does it open? When does it close?

2. On my vacation, I like to _____.

3. My neighborhood is _____.

4. Education is important because _____

   _____.

5. Jay's parents wouldn't let him work after school. Do you think they were right? Explain your answer.

6. Do some students have to work after school? Explain your answer.

7. Do you think being a lifeguard is a good summer job? Explain your answer.

8. A lifeguard has to be a good swimmer. What else does a lifeguard have to be able to do?

MATCHING

Match the words in Column A with their definitions or descriptions in Column B. Print the letters on the blank lines.

Column A	Column B
_____ 1. patience	A. to make money
_____ 2. boo	B. to cook in an oven
_____ 3. really	C. a very smart person
_____ 4. bake	D. to say it's necessary
_____ 5. meal	E. very
_____ 6. require	F. parents and teachers need this
_____ 7. initials	G. we eat three a day
_____ 8. earn	H. to give special attention to
_____ 9. wiz	I. the first letters of a name
_____ 10. emphasize	J. to show we don't like something

7

Cars and Accidents

An Accident

Reread the dialog "An Accident" (page 135 of **The Salsa Is Hot**) before doing the dialog and word reviews.

DIALOG REVIEW

*If the sentence is true, write **T**. If it's false, write **F** and change it to a true statement.*

1. _____ Frank has a big problem.

   _____

2. _____ He had an accident in his father's car.

   _____

3. _____ He was hurt in the accident.

   _____

4. _____ It'll cost more than $2,000 to fix the car.

   _____

5. _____ The accident wasn't Frank's fault.

   _____

6. _____ His father will be very angry.

   _____

7. _____ Frank is going to lie to his father.

   _____

WORD REVIEW

Complete the sentences with these words.

damage	over	speed	truth	worse

1. Many drivers _____ on the new highway.
2. I feel _____ today. I'm going to call the doctor.
3. The suit cost _____ $200.
4. Marty said he wasn't drinking. I hope he's telling the _____.
5. The hurricane did a lot of _____ to Puerto Rico.

140

| fault | insurance | lying | trouble | hurt |

6. Sally told me she graduated from college, but she was _____ .

7. The airplane crash was not the pilot's _____ .

8. Tony is in _____ . He got into a fight in school.

9. The _____ company paid $3,000 to fix my car.

10. Veronica _____ her knee playing basketball.

A NEW DRIVER

WORD BANK

Everywhere means to be in every place.
Whenever means any time something happens.
Either means *also* when used after negative verbs.
Junk is something that has no value.

Complete the dialog with these words and practice it with a partner.

junk	own	everywhere	borrow
whenever	license	either	

Charley and Andrea are married. They have a 17-year-old daughter who just got her driver's license. Her name is Courtney.

Charley: It's nice that Courtney has her _____.

Andrea: Yes and no.

Charley: What do you mean?

Andrea: Well, it's nice not to have to drive her _____.

Charley: True—she can drive herself to soccer practice.

Andrea: And to see her friends.

Charley: What's the bad part?

Andrea: I worry _____ she drives.

Charley: Do you know she wants to buy her _____ car?

Andrea: That's impossible. She doesn't have the money, and we don't _____.

Charley: She can buy a used car for $400.

Andrea: Any car you buy for $400 is _____. It won't be safe.

Charley: You're right. If she needs a car, she'll have to _____ ours.

WRITING A DIALOG

Work with a partner and create your own dialog. Give your dialog a title.

_____

A: I'm in big trouble.

B: What's the problem?

A: _____

B: _____

A: _____

B: _____

A: _____

B: _____

A: _____

SHARING INFORMATION

Discuss or complete these statements and questions. Use your imagination to complete the sentences in questions 1 and 2.

1. I _____ and it was my

    fault. I _____.

2. I'm in big trouble. I _____.

3. Do you think that teenage drivers speed more than others? If so, why?

4. Teenage drivers have to pay more for their car insurance. Why?

5. Is it fair that they have to pay more? Explain your answer.

6. Do you think parents should make teenage drivers pay for part or all of their car insurance? Explain your answer. If you are a teenage driver, do you pay for part or all of your car insurance?

7. Frank said that lying only makes things worse. Do you agree? Explain your answer.

8. Do you think that any car that costs $400 is junk? Explain your answer.

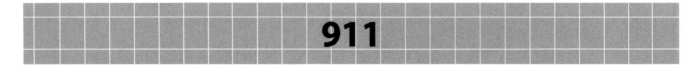

911

Reread the dialog "911" (page 138 of **The Salsa Is Hot**) before doing the dialog and word reviews.

DIALOG REVIEW

Answer these questions about the dialog. Use your own ideas to answer the last question.

1. What happened to Don? _____

2. Who called 911? _____

3. What did Don's mom do? _____

4. What did Don hurt when he hit the tree? _____

5. Is he conscious? Is he breathing? _____

6. Where is he? _____

7. What did Jeff tell Kate to do? _____

8. Why did he tell her not to move Don? _____

   _____

WORD REVIEW

Complete the sentences with these words.

blocks	on the way	bottom	conscious	rides

1. Vijay lives in New York City and _____ the subway every day.

2. The dog likes to sleep at the _____ of my bed.

3. It's only five _____ to the bus stop.

4. Alexandra fell on the stairs and hit her head, but she's still _____

5. I called 911, and the fire engines are _____.

breathe	quickly	bleeding	hill	blanket

6.   Chung read the newspaper _____ and went to work.

7. & 8. It was hard for me to _____ after I ran up the _____.

9.   I love this _____. It's soft and warm.

10.   The little girl fell on the sidewalk, and her knee is _____.

DON IS HURT!

The paragraphs below retell the dialog in the form of a story. Complete the paragraphs with these words.

quickly	breathing	911	hill
bleeding	blanket	riding	block

Don was _____ his bike down a _____ and hit a tree. His sister, Kate, shouted to their mom, and she came _____. She told Kate to call _____, and she ran to help Don.

Jeff answered Kate's call. She told him about the accident and that Don cut his head and was _____. Although he wasn't conscious, Don was _____.

Kate gave Jeff her address and told him that her brother was half a _____ away. Jeff told her to put a _____ on him and not to move him.

WORD GROUPS

Circle the three words or phrases that go together.

1.	speeding	driving	fast	quickly
2.	on the way	coming	soon	willing
3.	cheap	wrong	fault	bad
4.	bike	car	ride	bus
5.	911	emergency	accident	sorry
6.	conscious	pleased	awake	know

SHARING INFORMATION

Discuss these questions with a partner.

1. Don was not wearing a helmet. Do you think a helmet would have helped much?

2. Why do you think he went off the road?

3. What do you think his mother tried to do when she got to him?

4. Some people can't stand seeing blood. Does the sight of blood bother you? Does it bother you a lot?

5. Do you think Don stopped riding his bike because of the accident? Explain your answer.

6. Do you think a 911 operator has an interesting job? Is it a job you would like? Explain your answers.

7. If you go to school, do you ride or walk? If you ride, what do you ride—a car, a bus, a bike?

8. How many blocks is it from your house to your school?

Quiet, Roomy, and Safe

*Reread the dialog "Quiet, Roomy, and Safe" (page 141 of **The Salsa Is Hot**) before doing the dialog and word reviews.*

DIALOG REVIEW

*If the sentence is true, write **T**. If it's false, write **F** and change it to a true statement.*

1. _____ Kim Woo likes his Camry a lot.

   _____

2. _____ He knows the Camry is safe because Toyota did crash tests on it.

   _____

3. _____ Mi Cha likes the seats in Kim Woo's Camry.

   _____

4. _____ The trunk isn't big enough.

   _____

5. _____ Kim Woo had to pay extra for antilock brakes.

   _____

6. _____ Mi Cha thinks the Camry was expensive.

   _____

7. _____ Kim Woo and Mi Cha think it was worth the price.

   _____

WORD REVIEW

Complete the sentences with these words.

room	hopped	crash	comfortable	brakes

1. Three people were hurt in the bus _____.

2. How much will new _____ cost?

3. Luke _____ into the taxi and told the driver where to go.

4. This chair is very _____.

5. The elevator has _____ for ten people.

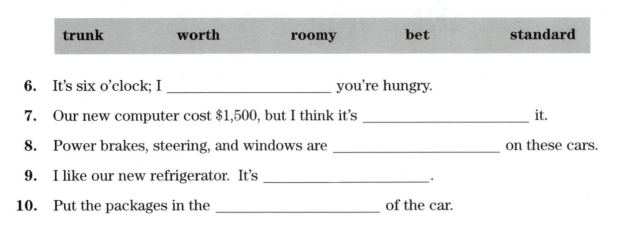

trunk	worth	roomy	bet	standard

6.   It's six o'clock; I _____ you're hungry.

7.   Our new computer cost $1,500, but I think it's _____ it.

8.   Power brakes, steering, and windows are _____ on these cars.

9.   I like our new refrigerator. It's _____.

10. Put the packages in the _____ of the car.

BUYING A USED CAR

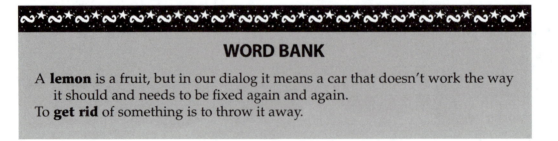

WORD BANK

A **lemon** is a fruit, but in our dialog it means a car that doesn't work the way
it should and needs to be fixed again and again.
To **get rid** of something is to throw it away.

Complete the dialog with these words and practice it with a partner.

so	worth	owe	get rid of
afford	lemon	trust	

Todd and Megan are cousins.

Todd: I have to buy a car.

Megan: How much will a new car cost?

Todd: Around $20,000, but I can't _____ it.

Megan: Why not?

Todd: We _____ too much on our credit cards and house.

Megan: You'll have to buy a used one.

Todd: I guess _____, but I don't like the idea.

Megan: Why not?

Todd: Ten years ago I bought a used car. It was a _____.

Megan: What was wrong with it?

Todd: A lot of things. I had to _____ it.

Megan: You can always get a mechanic to check the car.

Todd: Maybe I should. How much will that cost?

Megan: About $100.

Todd: It's _____ it. I need a car I can _____.

WRITING A DIALOG

Work with a partner and create your own dialog. Give your dialog a title.

_____

A: I have to buy a car.

B: _____

A: _____

B: _____

A: _____

B: _____

A: _____

B: _____

DICTATION

1.   *Listen while the teacher or your partner reads the dialog without stopping.*
     Don't write anything.
2.   *The teacher or your partner will read the dialog a second time, pausing after
     the missing lines.* **Write in the missing lines.**
3.   *The teacher or your partner will read the dialog a third time.* **Check your work.**

Megan: How much will a new car cost?

Todd: _____

Megan: Why not?

Todd: _____

Megan: You'll have to buy a used one.

Todd: _____

Megan: Why not?

Todd: _____

The Ax Slipped

Reread the dialog "The Ax Slipped," (page 144 of **The Salsa Is Hot**) before doing the dialog and word reviews.

DIALOG REVIEW

Answer these questions about the dialog. Use your own ideas to answer the last question.

1. Where did Bill's mom take him? _____

2. Why did she take him there? _____

3. What was he doing with the ax? _____

4. How bad is the cut? _____

5. Why will Bill need stitches? _____

6. What will he probably have from the cut? _____

7. What did Bill's dad do when Brian called him? _____

8. Do you think most people will notice Bill's scar? Explain your answer. _____

    _____

WORD REVIEW

Complete the sentences with these words.

ax	slipped	yard	definitely	wrong

1. Mr. Rana has a beautiful garden in his _____.

2. Be careful with that _____! You could hurt yourself.

3. You look upset. Is something _____?

4. I _____ on the kitchen floor and almost fell. It was wet.

5. Are you _____ going to Colombia this summer?

immediately	chopping	scar	pretty	stitches

6. This camera is _____ good.

7. The farmer is _____ down a tree.

8. The _____ stopped the bleeding.

9. I took the check to the bank _____.

10. The operation is going to leave a _____ on my neck.

A DOG BITE

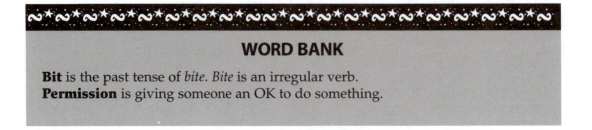

WORD BANK

Bit is the past tense of *bite*. *Bite* is an irregular verb.
Permission is giving someone an OK to do something.

Complete the dialog with these words and practice it with a partner.

hurry	permission	bit	emergency
stitches	matter	way	

Tom is Mrs. Sullivan's husband. Edward is their son. Dr. Mohamed phones the Sullivans.

Dr. Mohamed: Is this Mrs. Sullivan?

Mrs. Sullivan: Yes, it is.

Dr. Mohamed: I'm Doctor Mohamed of City Hospital.

Mrs. Sullivan: Did something happen to my mother?

Dr. Mohamed: No, but your son, Edward, is here. A dog _____ him.

Mrs. Sullivan: Oh, no! How is he?

Dr. Mohamed: There's nothing to worry about, but he needs _____.

Mrs. Sullivan: I'll be there in five minutes.

Dr. Mohamed: Good. We need your _____ to treat him.

Mrs. Sullivan: I'm on my _____.

Dr. Mohamed: Go to the _____ room. I'll meet you there. Bye.

Mrs. Sullivan: Tom! Tom! Get your coat. _____!

Tom: What's the _____? Why are you so upset?

Mrs. Sullivan: Eddie is in the emergency room of City Hospital. A dog bit him.

Tom: Calm down! He'll be OK. Let me drive.

Mrs. Sullivan: All right. Let's go!

WORD GROUPS

Circle the three words that go together.

1.	lemon	old-fashioned	junk	no good
2.	check	examine	look at	find
3.	allow	OK	decide	let
4.	cut	bleeding	stitches	crash
5.	clearly	completely	definitely	certainly
6.	dangerous	ambulance	hospital	accident

SHARING INFORMATION

Discuss or complete these statements and questions.

1. My _____ cost _____, but it was worth it.

2. Do you think it is very important to have anti-lock brakes? Explain your answer.

3. Do you (or your parents) use credit cards? Are they used a lot in your country?

4. _____ is definitely _____.

5. When I get home from school (work), I immediately _____

   _____.

6. (Remember that *pretty* here means "very." Complete *one* of these sentences.)

   I am pretty _____ . *or* I am a pretty _____.

7. Did a dog ever bite you? If so, how did it happen? Was the bite bad? What did you do for it?

8. How do we know that the Sullivans live near City Hospital?

The Titanic

Reread the story "The Titanic" (page 147 of **The Salsa Is Hot***) before doing the Story Review, Word Review, and Word and Story Review.*

STORY REVIEW

If the sentence is true, write **T**. *If it's false, write* **F** *and change it to a true statement.*

1. _____ In April 1912, the *Titanic* sailed from England and headed for New York City.
   _____

2. _____ She was the largest ship in the world, and this was her second voyage.
   _____

3. _____ Many of her passengers were rich and famous.
   _____

4. _____ The first-class passengers didn't mix with the other passengers.
   _____

5. _____ All the rooms on the *Titanic* were very large and expensive.
   _____

6. _____ Most of the third-class passengers were from the United States.
   _____

7. _____ Captain Smith didn't realize that there were icebergs in the area.
   _____

8. _____ No one could see very far because there was no moon.
   _____

WORD REVIEW

Complete the sentences with these words.

several	far	luxury	warning	couples

1. On every pack of cigarettes, there is a _____ about the dangers of smoking.

2. I drive to work every day. It's too _____ to walk.

3. Aaron invited five _____ to the party.

4. A Mercedes-Benz is a _____ car.

5. I asked the doctor _____ questions.

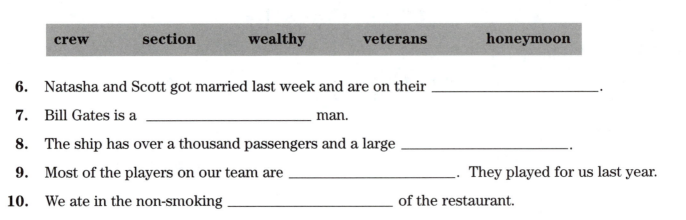

crew	section	wealthy	veterans	honeymoon

6.   Natasha and Scott got married last week and are on their _____.

7.   Bill Gates is a _____ man.

8.   The ship has over a thousand passengers and a large _____.

9.   Most of the players on our team are _____. They played for us last year.

10. We ate in the non-smoking _____ of the restaurant.

WORD AND STORY REVIEW

Complete the dialog with these words and practice it with a partner.

luxury	knots	veteran	icebergs	crew
wealthy	warnings	sections	far	couples

There Was No Moon

J. Bruce Ismay was the director of the White Star Line, which owned the *Titanic*. He was on the *Titanic* and lived to tell of the voyage. A reporter is talking to Mr. Ismay.

Reporter: Who was the captain of the *Titanic?*

Ismay: Captain Smith, a _____ of 38 years at sea.

Reporter: How many passengers were on the ship?

Ismay: Over 1,300, including 13 _____ on their honeymoon.

Reporter: Were all the passengers _____?

Ismay: No, most of those in the third-class _____ were immigrants.

Reporter: I imagine the first-class passengers lived in _____.

Ismay: Yes, they had a swimming pool, large rooms, and a fancy dining room.

Reporter: Did Captain Smith know there were _____ in the area?

Ismay: Yes, he received several _____ about them.

Reporter: Didn't that worry him or the _____?

Ismay: No, they continued to speed along at 22 _____ an hour.

Reporter: But why didn't they slow down?

Ismay: They thought they would be able to go around any iceberg they saw.

Reporter: Was the weather bad?

Ismay: No, the sea was calm, but there was no moon. No one could see very _____.

WRITING

Write a composition about a serious accident, fire, hurricane, or earthquake you were in. Or, if you prefer, write a summary of the story of the Titanic. Emphasize the second part of the story which is on page 151 of **The Salsa Is Hot**. *Leave out all unnecessary details and write the summary in your own words as much as possible.*

Iceberg Ahead

Reread the story "Iceberg Ahead" (page 151 of **The Salsa Is Hot***) before doing the Story Review, Word Review, and Word and Story Review.*

STORY REVIEW

If the sentence is true, write **T***. If it's false, write* **F** *and change it to a true statement.*

1. _____ The sailors who were on lookout warned Captain Smith.

   _____

2. _____ First Officer Murdock tried to go around the iceberg.

   _____

3. _____ The *Titanic* hit the iceberg at 11:40 P.M. and began to fill up with water.

   _____

4. _____ It was a long time before Captain Smith realized that the *Titanic* was in trouble.

   _____

5. _____ The crew put all the passengers into lifeboats.

   _____

6. _____ The *Carpathia* arrived just before the *Titanic* sank.

   _____

7. _____ The *Carpathia* rescued 705 people from the lifeboats.

   _____

8. _____ Many passengers and crew members drowned.

   _____

WORD REVIEW

Complete the sentences with these words.

ahead	drowned	lifeboats	as hot as	loading

1. Two boys were swimming in the river. One of them _____ .

2. Is today going to be _____ yesterday?

3. There is a beautiful lake two miles _____ .

4. They're _____ the packages on the truck.

5. I'm glad to see that our ship has _____ .

158

suddenly	lower	sank	rescued	slow down

6.   I hit the golf ball into the water, and it _____.

7.   You're walking too fast. Please _____.

8.   Someone _____ shouted "Fire!" and everyone left the building.

9.   The baby fell into the pool, but his father _____ him.

10.   The picture on the wall is too high. _____ it a little.

WORD AND STORY REVIEW

Complete the dialog with these words and practice it with a partner.

loaded	as fast as	bridge	unsinkable	lookout
sink	drowned	lifeboats	rescue	heading

A Call for Help

After the *Carpathia* landed in New York, Senator William Smith questioned some of the passengers and crew members of the *Titanic*. One of those he questioned was J. Bruce Ismay, the director of the White Star Line.

Smith: Mr. Ismay, I trust you won't mind answering my questions about the *Titanic*.

Ismay: Not at all, Senator.

Smith: Who first saw the iceberg?

Ismay: The two sailors on _____.

Smith: What did they do?

Ismay: They warned First Officer Murdock. He was on the _____.

Smith: He must have tried to go around the iceberg.

Ismay: Yes, but the side of the *Titanic* hit the iceberg, and the ship began to fill with water.

Smith: Did the captain realize the ship was going to _____?

Ismay: Yes, and the crew began putting the passengers in the _____.

Smith: I understand you didn't have enough of them.

Ismay: No, we didn't. That's why we _____ women and children in first.

Smith: What was the name of the ship that came to help?

Ismay: The *Carpathia*. She was _____ for the Mediterranean when she heard the call for help.

Smith: Didn't she also have to worry about icebergs?

Ismay: Yes, but she came _____ possible.

Smith: How many people did she _____?

Ismay: Seven hundred and five.

Smith: What happened to the other passengers and crew members?

Ismay: They _____ in the Atlantic Ocean.

Smith: Why didn't the *Titanic* have more lifeboats?

Ismay: We thought the ship was _____.

SHARING INFORMATION

Discuss or complete these statements and questions.

1.   I am as _____ as _____.

2.   Do you think the crew of the *Titanic* was proud to be working on the ship? Explain your answer.

3.   Why was it very difficult for the crew to communicate with many third-class passengers?

4.   The *Titanic* sank on April 15 in the North Atlantic. How cold do you think the water was? Explain your answer.

5.   Name as many things as you can that we have today that would make crossing the Atlantic safer than in 1912.

6.   How safe would you feel in a lifeboat in the middle of the Atlantic Ocean?

7.   What new law or laws do you think were passed because of the sinking of the *Titanic*?

8.   What do you think the sinking of the *Titanic* teaches us about life?

MATCHING

Match the words in Column A with their definitions or descriptions in Column B.
Print the letters on the blank lines.

Column A	Column B
_____ 1. license	A. a separate part
_____ 2. suddenly	B. at any time
_____ 3. get rid of	C. to save from danger
_____ 4. whenever	D. you need one to drive
_____ 5. junk	E. also (used after negative verbs)
_____ 6. far	F. to throw away
_____ 7. section	G. the workers on a ship
_____ 8. rescue	H. at a great distance
_____ 9. crew	I. happening without warning
_____ 10. either	J. something with no value

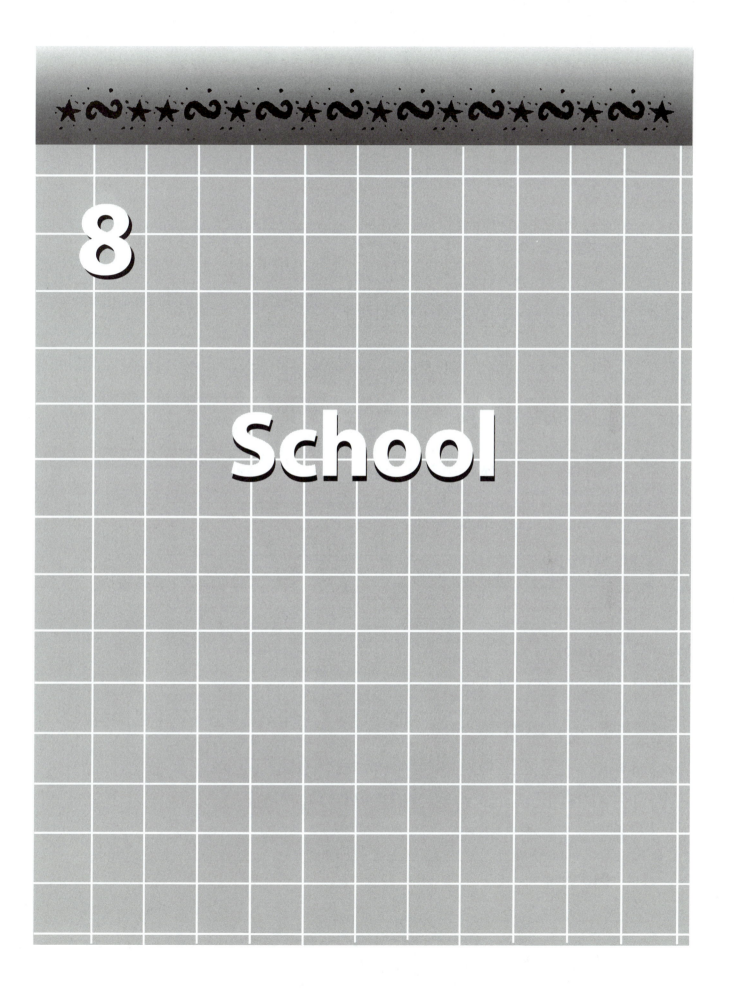

8

School

The First Day of School

Reread the dialog "The First Day of School" (page 157 of **The Salsa Is Hot**) before doing the dialog and word reviews.

DIALOG REVIEW

If the sentence is true, write **T**. If it's false, write **F** and change it to a true statement.

1. _____ Marina wants fall to begin.

_____

2. _____ Alexi doesn't want summer to end.

_____

3. _____ It's his second year in high school.

_____

4. _____ He knows some English.

_____

5. _____ He needs a class for beginners.

_____

6. _____ Marina likes most of her teachers.

_____

7. _____ Alexi doesn't mind homework.

_____

WORD REVIEW

Complete the sentences with these words.

wow	so	over	first	hate

1. Lin was my _____ girlfriend, and I still like her.

2. It's Saturday, _____ I don't have to work.

3. The kids _____ to go to bed.

4. & 5. That suit costs _____ $400. _____, that's expensive!

| worry | beginner | so | a lot of | ends |

6. Jack plays the piano, and _____ do I.

7. Don't tell me how the story _____.

8. For a _____, Courtney is a good golfer.

9. The school band is excellent. They spend _____ time practicing.

10. I _____ about my brother. He's losing weight and doesn't feel well.

BE FAIR, BE PATIENT, BE THE BOSS!

WORD BANK

Nervous means *afraid*.
Understandable means easy to understand.
Advice is an opinion you give someone about what to do.
To **expect** is to think that something will happen or that someone will do something.

Complete the dialog with these words and practice it with a partner.

expect	either	nervous	understandable
advice	veteran	let	

Katie and Brett are teachers. This is Katie's first day as a teacher.

Katie: How long have you been teaching?

Brett: Twenty-five years! I'm a _____.

Katie: And this is my first day. I'm a little _____.

Brett: That's _____.

Katie: Do you have any _____?

Brett: Yes, be serious and make sure you're in control.

Katie: I will. Don't worry about that.

Brett: _____ you control the class, or the class will control you.

Katie: I can't _____ that happen.

Brett: _____ a lot, and you'll get a lot.

Katie: And if I don't, I'll get nothing.

Brett: Or very little. Be fair, be patient, and be the boss!

Katie: I like your suggestions.

Brett: Good luck!

Katie: Thank you!

WRITING A DIALOG

Work with a partner and create your own dialog. Give your dialog a title.

_____

A: Tomorrow is the first day of school.

B: _____

A: _____

B: _____

A: _____

B: _____

A: _____

B: _____

HOW IMPORTANT IS IT?

Circle the number that tells how important you think each quality is in a teacher. Compare your answers with those of a partner.

> 1 = not that important
>
> 2 = important
>
> 3 = very important
>
> 4 = very, very important

A.	Be fair.	1	2	3	4
B.	Be patient.	1	2	3	4
C.	Be polite.	1	2	3	4
D.	Be easy to talk to.	1	2	3	4
E.	Be interesting (not boring).	1	2	3	4
F.	Be able to control the class.	1	2	3	4
G.	Like to teach.	1	2	3	4
H.	Know well the subject he/she teaches.	1	2	3	4
I.	Expect a lot of the students.	1	2	3	4

Old-Fashioned

Reread the dialog "Old-Fashioned" (page 160 of **The Salsa Is Hot**) before doing the dialog and word reviews.

DIALOG REVIEW

Answer these questions about the dialog. Use your own ideas to answer the last question.

1. What does Miss Walker teach? _____

2. When did Amy have her? _____

3. Why does Amy say Miss Walker is old-fashioned? _____

   _____

4. How does Miss Walker hide her sense of humor? _____

5. Why does Dave say she's fair? _____

6. How does she sound to him? _____

7. What do Miss Walker's students have to do? _____

8. Would you like to have Miss Walker as a teacher? Explain your answer. _____

   _____

   _____

WORD REVIEW

Complete the sentences with these words.

ever	hide	marks	old-fashioned	so

1. I like that sweater, and it's not _____ expensive.

2. Leslie got a D in math, but all her other _____ were good.

3. Do you _____ play cards?

4. Our school has a young principal, but some of his ideas are _____.

5. I'll be happy to answer your questions. I have nothing to _____.

discussion	deserved	sense of humor	boring	sounds

6. Gabe doesn't have a _____. He's too serious.

7. Your trip _____ great.

8. Our team played hard. They _____ to win.

9. Derek and Kristen had a _____ about his job.

10. My wife liked the show, but I thought it was _____.

LOTS OF TESTS AND HOMEWORK

The paragraphs below retell the dialog in the form of a story. Complete the paragraphs with these words.

sound	deserve	old-fashioned	mark
discussion	hides	fair	sense of humor

Miss Walker is Dave's history teacher, and Amy had her last year. Amy thinks Miss Walker is _____ because there is not much _____ in her class, and she gives homework every night and lots of tests.

Miss Walker has a _____, but she _____ it at first by not smiling until Thanksgiving.

She gives you the _____ you _____, nothing more and nothing less, which is _____. She's never boring and you learn a lot in her class. She doesn't _____ so bad.

WORD GROUPS

Circle the three words or phrases that go together

1.	summer	July	spring	winter
2.	patient	calm	peaceful	wonderful
3.	kind	smile	laugh	sense of humor
4.	a lot of	much	any	many
5.	advice	opinion	decision	suggestion
6.	teach	believe in	show	train

SHARING INFORMATION

Discuss these questions with a partner.

1. What advice would you give a new teacher?

2. Is teaching a good job? Explain your answer.

3. Do you think you would like to be a teacher? Explain your answer.

4. Do you have enough patience to be a teacher? Explain your answer.

5. Are most of your classes interesting? Do you like school? Explain your answer.

6. Do you think you get the marks you deserve? Explain your answer.

7. Do you ever complain about your teachers? If so, why do you complain?

8. Do you think you have a good sense of humor?

Writing Is Tough Work

Reread the dialog "Writing Is Tough Work" (page 163 of **The Salsa Is Hot**) before doing the dialog and word reviews.

DIALOG REVIEW

If the sentence is true, write **T**. If it's false, write **F** and change it to a true statement.

1. _____ Mike is reading about Japan in an encyclopedia.

   _____

2. _____ He has to do a report for his history class.

   _____

3. _____ Reading about Japan is interesting for him.

   _____

4. _____ He doesn't like writing reports.

   _____

5. _____ Debbie thinks writing is difficult.

   _____

6. _____ Mike doesn't mind working.

   _____

7. _____ He gets angry when Debbie calls him "lazybones."

   _____

WORD REVIEW

Complete the sentences with these words.

geography	mind	tough	surprise	guess

1. Do you _____ driving me to the bank? My car won't start.

2. The doctor told Jamie she was going to have twins. It was a big _____.

3. Our _____ book has a chapter on the lakes and rivers of North America.

4. The baby is crying. I _____ she's hungry.

5. Three colleges accepted Enrique. He has to choose one. It's a _____ decision.

| choices | lazybones | means | report | encyclopedia |

6. The C.I.A. sent the president a secret _____ on Russia.

7. You sleep too much, _____.

8. I'm reading an article about the Pilgrims in an _____.

9. The store has so many computers. You have a lot of _____ if you want to buy one.

10. Our science teacher isn't very clear. Sometimes I don't know what he _____.

IDEAS COME FIRST

Writing is sharing ideas

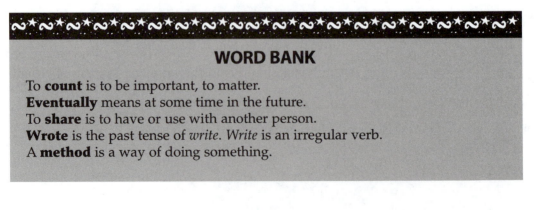

WORD BANK

To **count** is to be important, to matter.
Eventually means at some time in the future.
To **share** is to have or use with another person.
Wrote is the past tense of *write*. *Write* is an irregular verb.
A **method** is a way of doing something.

Complete the dialog with these words and practice it with a partner.

eventually	wrote	counts	method
emphasize	mistakes	sharing	

Vicky and Eric are high-school teachers and friends.

Vicky: What are you teaching this year?

Eric: Writing.

Vicky: That's tough. How do you do it?

Eric: I _____ what students have to say, their ideas.

Vicky: So you don't care about grammar and spelling.

Eric: Yes, I do. Everything _____, but ideas come first.

Vicky: Do you correct their grammar _____?

Eric: _____, but first I comment on what they have to say.

Vicky: Do the students like that?

Eric: Sure, they see that writing is _____ ideas. And it can be fun.

Vicky: You probably have the students work in pairs.

Eric: Yes, and before they write, they discuss their ideas with their partner.

Vicky: And after they write?

Eric: Their partner reads what they _____ and comments on it.

Vicky: It sounds like a good _____.

Eric: I think so.

WRITING A DIALOG

Work with a partner and create your own dialog. Give your dialog a title.

_____

A: What are you reading?

B: _____

A: _____

B: _____

A: _____

B: _____

DICTATION

1. *Listen while the teacher or your partner reads the dialog without stopping.* **Don't write anything.**
2. *The teacher or your partner will read the dialog a second time, pausing after the missing lines.* **Write in the missing lines.**
3. *The teacher or your partner will read the dialog a third time.* **Check your work.**

Vicky: Do you correct their grammar mistakes?

Eric: _____

Vicky: Do the students like that?

Eric: _____

Vicky: You probably have the students work in pairs.

Eric: _____

Vicky: And after they write?

Eric: _____

A Million Rules

Reread the dialog "A Million Rules" (page 166 of **The Salsa Is Hot**) before doing the dialog and word reviews.

DIALOG REVIEW

Answer these questions about the dialog. Use your own ideas to answer the last question.

1. Why is Shawn unhappy? _____

2. Why did Mr. Williams give him detention? _____

3. Why does Shawn say that Mr. Williams is too much? _____

4. What are three of Mr. Williams's rules? _____
   _____

5. What is the difference between many other teachers and Mr. Williams? _____
   _____

6. How does he enforce his rules? _____
   _____

7. What does Laura think of him? _____

8. Do you think Mr. Williams is too much? Explain your answer _____
   _____

WORD REVIEW

Complete the sentences with these words.

throw	rules	gum	yells	seats

1. _____ has a lot of sugar and isn't good for our teeth.

2. The bus has 45 _____.

3. The umpire has to know the _____ of the game.

4. Mrs. Florio _____ at the children when they play in her garden.

5. The paper plates are dirty. _____ them in the garbage.

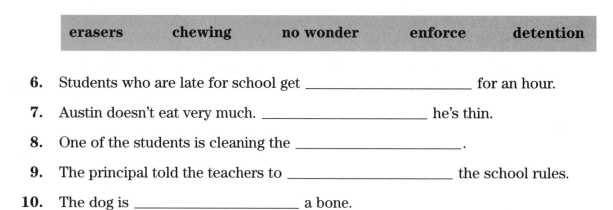

| erasers | chewing | no wonder | enforce | detention |

6. Students who are late for school get _____ for an hour.

7. Austin doesn't eat very much. _____ he's thin.

8. One of the students is cleaning the _____.

9. The principal told the teachers to _____ the school rules.

10. The dog is _____ a bone.

ZERO

TEST TODAY

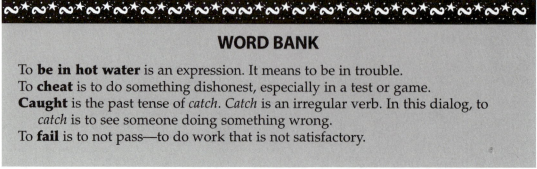

WORD BANK

To **be in hot water** is an expression. It means to be in trouble.
To **cheat** is to do something dishonest, especially in a test or game.
Caught is the past tense of *catch*. *Catch* is an irregular verb. In this dialog, to *catch* is to see someone doing something wrong.
To **fail** is to not pass—to do work that is not satisfactory.

Complete the dialog with these words and practice it with a partner.

fail	enough	upset	cheating
couple	hot water	caught	

Marty and Gloria are high-school students and friends.

Marty: I'm in _____.

Gloria: What happened?

Marty: I was _____ on my science test.

Gloria: And the teacher _____ you.

Marty: Exactly. I had some notes under my paper.

Gloria: What did the teacher do?

Marty: He took my paper and gave me a zero.

Gloria: Are you going to _____ for the marking period?

Marty: Yes, and my parents are going to be _____ and angry.

Gloria: What will they say?

Marty: I can't go out for a _____ of weeks.

Gloria: That's not so bad.

Marty: It's bad _____.

WORD GROUPS

Circle the three words that go together.

1. caring   thinking   sharing   giving

2. mistake   error   wrong   waste

3. deserve   be important   count   matter

4. math   history   geography   social studies

5. Japan   China   Canada   India

6. speaking   resting   reading   writing

SHARING INFORMATION

Discuss these questions with a partner.

1. In the past, all encyclopedias were books. Today encyclopedias come on CD-ROMs. What are the advantages of the CD-ROMs?

2. What are the advantages of books?

3. If you want to use an encylopedia, do you prefer to use a book or a CD-ROM? Explain your answer.

4. The dialog "Ideas Come First" says that grammar and spelling are important but that the ideas in a composition are more important. Do you agree? Explain your answer.

5. Writing is "sharing ideas." What does that mean?

6. Do you think it helps to have another student, a partner, read your composition and comment on it? Explain your answer.

7. When Marty's science teacher caught him cheating, the teacher took his paper and gave Marty a zero. Do you think the teacher did the right thing? Explain your answer.

8. What do most teachers do if they catch a student cheating? What would you do if you were a teacher?

More Opportunities

*Reread the story "More Opportunities" (page 169 of **The Salsa Is Hot**) before doing the Story Review, Word Review, and Word and Story Review.*

STORY REVIEW

*If the sentence is true, write **T**. If it's false, write **F** and change it to a true statement.*

1. _____ Nicole was born in a small village near Port-au-Prince, Haiti.

   _____

2. _____ Nicole's father was a carpenter and had no trouble finding work.

   _____

3. _____ Nicole was an intelligent girl, and history was her favorite subject.

   _____

4. _____ She liked to read.

   _____

5. _____ She was happy her father was going to the United States.

   _____

6. _____ He went to the United States to look for work and to make a lot of money.

   _____

7. _____ He promised to bring the whole family to the United States.

   _____

8. _____ The day Nicole flew to the United States was one of the happiest of her life.

   _____

WORD REVIEW

Complete the sentences with these words.

bright	village	promised	steady	carpenter

1. Diana spends a lot of money in our store. She's a _____ customer.

2. Rashad is the best student in our class. He's _____.

3. I _____ to take the children to the parade.

4. Gino is a very good _____. He makes kitchen cabinets.

5. There is only one store in the _____.

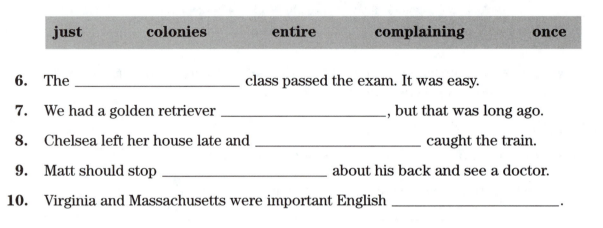

just	colonies	entire	complaining	once

6. The _____ class passed the exam. It was easy.

7. We had a golden retriever _____, but that was long ago.

8. Chelsea left her house late and _____ caught the train.

9. Matt should stop _____ about his back and see a doctor.

10. Virginia and Massachusetts were important English _____.

WORD AND STORY REVIEW

Complete the dialog with these words and practice it with a partner.

colony	promised	carpenter	Creole	steady
bright	opportunities	village	complained	just

A New Student

Rachel is a guidance counselor who talked to Nicole, and Brad is going to be her ESL teacher.

Rachel: You're getting a new student tomorrow. Her name is Nicole.

Brad: Where is she from?

Rachel: A small _____ in Haiti. It's _____ outside of Port-au-Prince.

Brad: I don't know much about Haiti.

Rachel: It was once a French _____.

Brad: What's her first language?

Rachel: Haitian _____. She also knows some French.

Brad: Is she a good student?

Rachel: Very. She's a _____ girl and loves math.

Brad: Do you know anything about her family?

Rachel: Her father is a _____.

Brad: When did he come to the United States?

Rachel: He came two years ago to find _____ work.

Brad: And he left his family in Haiti.

Rachel: Yes, but he _____ to bring them to the United States.

Brad: Is Nicole happy to be here?

Rachel: No, she _____ to her mother about leaving Haiti.

Brad: What did her mother say?

Rachel: That she would have more _____ in the United States.

Brad: She should.

WRITING

Imagine that a couple born in the United States, who are good friends of yours, wish to visit your country for a week at the end of June. Write them a letter telling them about the places they should visit, what the weather will be like and the clothing they should take, where they might stay, and anything special they should know to enjoy their visit.

Dear _____,

_____

_____

_____

_____

_____

_____

_____

_____

_____

_____

_____

_____

_____

_____

A Dream Come True

Reread the story "A Dream Come True" (page 173 of **The Salsa Is Hot**) before doing the Story Review, Word Review, and Word and Story Review.

STORY REVIEW

If the sentence is true, write **T**. If it's false, write **F** and change it to a true statement.

1. _____ Nicole started school in Brooklyn in September.

   _____

2. _____ At first, Nicole didn't like school.

   _____

3. _____ None of the teachers at her school spoke creole.

   _____

4. _____ The counselor didn't think she could go to college because her family couldn't afford it.

   _____

5. _____ The counselor told her of scholarships and grants she could apply for.

   _____

6. _____ Nicole graduated from Medgar Evers College with high honors.

   _____

7. _____ Nicole got a job as a bilingual (English/Haitian Creole) math teacher.

   _____

8. _____ The students like her class because she lets them do whatever they want.

   _____

WORD REVIEW

Complete the sentences with these words.

respect	strict	counselor	little by little	dream

1. The room is still cold, but it's getting warmer _____.

2. Our boss is very _____, but I like her.

3. Ted's _____ is to be a great actor.

4. A _____ is helping Tyler with his drinking problem.

5. I have a lot of _____ for firefighters.

fortunately	grant	proud	afford	bilingual

6. Rebecca is applying for a government _____ to go to a two-year college.

7. It's a beautiful dress, but I can't _____ it.

8. Joe fell off his bike. _____, he was wearing a helmet and is OK.

9. Canada is a _____ country. English and French are its official languages.

10. Our daughter is a very good tennis player. We're _____ of her.

WORD AND STORY REVIEW

Complete the dialog with these words and practice it with a partner.

grants	hated	bilingual	counselor	afford
fortunately	proud	little by little	strict	respect

A Good Teacher

Nicole is talking to her cousin Pierre. She hasn't seen him for many years.

Pierre: When you started school in the United States, how did you like it?

Nicole: At first, I _____ it.

Pierre: Why?

Nicole: The students didn't seem to have much _____ for the teachers.

Pierre: And in Haiti they have a lot.

Nicole: Exactly. _____, some students and one teacher knew creole.

Pierre: That must have helped.

Nicole: It did, and _____ things got better.

Pierre: Did you get good marks?

Nicole: Yes, and I wanted to go to college, but my parents couldn't _____ it.

Pierre: Didn't you know about scholarships and government _____?

Nicole: No, but I went to a _____, and she told me about them.

Pierre: So you went to college.

Nicole: Yes, I went to Medgar Evers and graduated with high honors.

Pierre: Your family must have been _____ of you.

Nicole: They were. Then I got a job as a _____math teacher.

Pierre: Do you like your job?

Nicole: I love it. I'm very _____, but the students know I want to help them.

Pierre: I bet you're a good teacher.

Nicole: I hope so.

WRITING

Write a composition comparing the schools in your country with those in the United States. Some of the things you may wish to compare are teachers, students, subjects studied, discipline, size of the schools, class size, and length of the school day.

MATCHING

Match the words in Column A with their definitions or descriptions in Column B. Print the letters on the blank lines.

	Column A	Column B
_____	**1.** nervous	**A.** in the past
_____	**2.** cheat	**B.** to be important
_____	**3.** method	**C.** not changing or stopping
_____	**4.** once	**D.** to be dishonest
_____	**5.** share	**E.** at some time in the future
_____	**6.** steady	**F.** of course
_____	**7.** mistake	**G.** afraid
_____	**8.** eventually	**H.** to use with another
_____	**9.** count	**I.** an error
_____	**10.** no wonder	**J.** a way of doing something

Word List

The words used in the sentence and dialog completion exercises and in the matching exercises are listed below.

A

a lot of *163*
about *59, 61, 62*
accountant *82, 92*
advice *163, 164*
afford *103, 149, 181*
again *108*
against *43*
age *85*
ago *19, 32, 82*
ahead *158*
allow *7*
along *22*
although *112*
angry *75*
annoy *104, 105*
answer *75*
any *27*
anymore *91, 92*
apply *15, 131*
argue *81, 104, 120, 122, 123*
argument *104*
around *51, 52, 105*
arrive *22*
as fast as *159*
as hot as *158*
astronaut *54*
at all *115*
at first *88, 89*
at least *23, 40, 76*
attractive *78, 79*
away *97, 98*
ax *151*

B

bake *7, 127*
balloon *58*
band *50*
bargain *39, 40*
bark *96*
basement *118*
beach *36*
beef *34*
beginner *163*
behave *11, 12*
believe *75*
believe in *34*
besides *6, 32, 55, 101, 123*
best *97, 129*
bet *14, 19, 74, 148*
better *7, 12, 126*

better off *75*
better than *127*
big shot *104*
bike *119*
bilingual *181*
bill *23*
bit (n.) *11, 12, 105*
bit (v.) (bite) *152, 153*
bite *97*
blanket *145*
bleed *145*
block *144, 145*
blood *28*
boo *119, 120*
boring *6, 52, 167*
borrow *61, 62, 109, 142*
bossy *81*
both *91, 92, 115*
bother *14*
bottom *144*
brakes *147*
breathe *145*
breeze *36*
bridge *159*
bright *177, 178*
broke (break) *75, 76*
by the way *79*

C

C.I.A. *130*
calm down *74*
candle *55*
candy *55*
career *43*
carpenter *177, 178*
catch (n.) *47*
catch (v.) *47, 174*
caught (catch) *174, 175*
celebrate *57*
celebration *70*
chat *91, 92, 115*
cheap *58, 59, 103, 129*
cheat *174, 175*
check (v.) *114, 115*
chef *130*
chew *174*
choice *78, 79, 170*
cholesterol *27, 28*
chop (down) *152*
close (adj.) *114*
coach *3, 4, 120*
colony *178*

comfortable *147*
company *7*
complain *103, 123, 178*
completely *8*
compromise *82*
concentrate *114, 115*
concert *92, 105*
congratulations *40*
conscious *144*
contract *43*
cookout *50*
couch *51, 52*
couch potato *51*
council *69, 70*
counselor *180, 181*
count *170, 171*
couple (two people) *155, 156*
couple (two things) *31, 32, 175*
courage *68*
crash (into) (v.) *47*
crash (n.) *147*
crazy about *42, 98*
creole *178*
crew *156*
cross *30*
cry (cries) *74*
customer *3*

D

damage *140*
dangerous *11, 30*
decide *64, 65*
definitely *151*
degree *35, 36*
deliver *14*
depend *39, 40*
deserve *167*
detention *174*
diamond *91, 92*
die (dying) *47*
difference *70*
diner *23*
discover *18*
discussion *167*
disturb *118*
dozen *85, 86*
dream *88, 89, 180*
drown *158, 159*

E

earn *134*
earrings *61, 62*
earthquake *47*
easier *97, 98*
either *134, 144, 142, 162*
elect *47*
emergency *76*
emergency room *75*
emphasize *137, 171*
encyclopedia *170*
end *163*
enforce *174*
engaged *19*
engagement *86*
engineering *136, 137*
enough *22, 31, 137, 175*
entire *38, 178*
entirely *38*
equator *19*
eraser *174*
especially *54*
even *111, 112*
eventually *170, 171*
ever *166*
everywhere *141, 142*
example *16*
excited *57, 59*
exercise *28, 34, 52*
expect *163, 164*
expensive *23, 59, 109*

F

factory *19*
fail *11, 12, 174, 175*
fair *74, 167*
fancy *103*
fantastic *62, 127*
far *51, 52, 155, 156*
fault *104, 105, 141*
favorite *8, 85, 86, 119*
feed *114, 115*
feel like *51, 52*
fell (fall) *75, 76*
few *18, 89*
finally *23*
find *19*
fire (v.) *14*
firehouse *126, 127*
fireworks *51*
first *162*